Oxford Progressive Engl
General Editor: D.F

GW00367012

The Good Ea

The *Oxford Progressive English Readers* series provides a wide range of reading for learners of English. It includes classics, the favourite stories of young readers, and also modern fiction. The series has five grades: the *Introductory Grade* at a 1400 word level, *Grade 1* at a 2100 word level, *Grade 2* at a 3100 word level, *Grade 3* at a 3700 word level and *Grade 4* which consists of abridged stories. Structural as well as lexical controls are applied at each level.

Wherever possible the mood and style of the original stories have been retained. Where this requires departure from the grading scheme, definitions and notes are given.

All the books in the series are attractively illustrated. Each book also has a short section containing questions and suggested activities for students.

The Good Earth

Pearl S. Buck

Hong Kong
OXFORD UNIVERSITY PRESS
Oxford Singapore Tokyo

Oxford University Press

Oxford New York Toronto
Petaling Jaya Singapore Hong Kong Tokyo
Delhi Bombay Calcutta Madras Karachi
Nairobi Dar es Salaam Cape Town
Melbourne Auckland
and associated companies in
Beirut Berlin Ibadan Nicosia

© *Oxford University Press 1980*
This adaptation first published 1980
Fifth impression 1985

The Good Earth first published in Great Britain 1931
by Methuen and Co. Ltd.

OXFORD is a trade mark of Oxford University Press

Retold by Emma Letley
Illustrated by the Illustration Workshop
Simplified according to the language grading scheme
especially compiled by D.H. Howe

ISBN 0 19 581035 X

Printed in Hong Kong by Hing Yip Printing Co. Ltd.
Published by Oxford University Press, Warwick House, Hong Kong

Contents

1 Wang Lung Goes to the House of Hwang

It was Wang Lung's wedding day. At first, when he woke up, he could not think why it was different from any other day. Then he remembered and jumped quickly out of bed. He looked out of a small hole in the wall of the house and heard a soft wind. This sound was a good omen*. Wang Lung knew   *5* that it would bring rain and the fields and crops needed rain badly. He got dressed, lit the fire and took some hot water to his old father. He had done this every day for six years and this was the last time. The next day his new wife would light the fire and heat the water.   *10*

Wang Lung went to his room and took a small bundle of grey cloth out of his belt. He counted the money and there were six silver dollars and some copper coins. He had not yet told his father that he had invited friends to supper in the evening. His male cousin, his uncle and three farmers were all   *15* coming to share his wedding supper. He planned to buy pork, a small pond fish and some chestnuts from the market. He might even buy a few bamboo shoots from the South and a little beef if there was enough money. Then he thought he would like to have his head shaved. That would take some of   *20* the money. Perhaps there would not be enough for all the food.

He left his father and went out into the early Spring morning. He walked among the fields along a narrow path. In the near distance he could see the grey wall of the city. Inside   *25* that wall was the great house where his future wife had been a slave since she was a child. 'We are too poor to afford a large wedding, gold rings and silk clothes,' his father had said. 'You will have to marry a slave woman. And I don't want you to marry a pretty, young slave. We must have a woman   *30*

*omen, a sign of something good or a warning of something bad.

who will look after the house and work in the fields. We are farmers and a pretty woman would be no use in our family.'

So one day his father had gone to the great House of Hwang and asked if there was a slave for his son. The mistress
5 of the house had told him that Wang Lung could marry O-Lan. Then Wang Lung's father had bought two silver rings washed in gold and a pair of silver earrings. He gave these to O-Lan's owner as a promise that Wang Lung would marry her slave. Wang Lung had never seen the woman and today he
10 was to go and fetch her from the House of Hwang.

He walked through the gate of the city and soon he was in the street of the barbers*. He had his head shaved and then he went to the market. The town people made him feel very foolish because he was a farmer and not used to their ways.
15 He walked to the gates of the great house but then he was filled with great terror. Perhaps he should not have come alone? Perhaps he should have asked his father or his uncle to come with him? Or even his neighbour Ching? He stood and looked at the gates for a long time. They were huge
20 wooden gates bound with iron and there were two stone lions beside them. There was no one else there. It was impossible. He was too nervous to go inside the gates.

He went to a small street-restaurant and ate a little and, at noon, returned to the House of Hwang. This time the gates
25 were not closed and the gatekeeper stood idly there. When he saw Wang Lung with his basket of food, he thought he had come to sell something at the great house. He shouted at him in a very rough voice. 'Now then, what do you want?'

Wang Lung replied with great difficulty. 'I am Wang Lung,
30 the farmer . . . I am come . . . I am come . . .'

'I can see that,' said the gatekeeper who was only polite to friends of his master and mistress.

'I have come to fetch a woman,' said Wang Lung nervously.

The man roared with laughter. He laughed and laughed and
35 Wang Lung felt very foolish indeed. 'I was told to expect a

*barber, a person whose trade is shaving and cutting men's hair.

bridegroom* today,' he said, 'but I did not recognize you. I didn't think a bridegroom would come with a basket of shopping on his arm.'

'It is only a little meat,' said Wang Lung and waited for the man to open the gates. But the gatekeeper did not move.   5

'Shall I go alone?' asked Wang Lung.

'No, no,' said the man, 'the Old Lord would kill you if you did that.' Then he saw how innocent Wang Lung was and realized that he did not know he should give money to him.

'A little silver is a good key.'   10

'I am only a poor man,' said Wang Lung unhappily.

'Well, let me see what you have in your belt.'

Then the gatekeeper laughed loudly as Wang Lung actually put down his basket and took the bag of money from his belt. He shook out the money into his hand and there was 15 one silver piece and fourteen copper coins.

'I will take the silver,' said the man in a very cold voice and, before Wang Lung could protest, he had put the silver in his sleeve. He marched through the gate shouting, 'The bridegroom! The bridegroom!'   20

*bridegroom, a man on the day of his marriage.

2 O-Lan

Wang Lung was very angry with the gatekeeper, but he had
to follow him. He walked through court after court hearing
the man's voice roaring in front of him. Then suddenly, after
it seemed as if he had walked through a hundred courts, the
5 gatekeeper was silent and pushed him into a little room. In a
few minutes he returned.

    'The Old Mistress says you are to appear before her,' he
said and led Wang Lung into a huge hall. In the middle of the
room there was a platform where an old lady lay. She had a
10 very small, fine body and a thin, lined face. Her eyes were
black and sharp as a monkey's eyes and she was dressed in a
satin* robe. On a low bench beside her there was a pipe of
opium* burning over a small lamp.

    Wang Lung dropped down on to his knees and knocked his
15 head on the floor in front of the great lady.

    'Let him get up from the floor,' she said to the gatekeeper.
'Has he come for the woman?'

    'Yes, Ancient One,' he replied.

    'Why doesn't he speak for himself?' she asked.

20   'Because he is a fool.'

    This made Wang Lung very angry with the man and he
looked at him crossly. 'I am only a rough farmer,' he said to
the old lady, 'and I do not know how to speak to a great lady
like yourself, Ancient One.'

25   'Call O-Lan quickly,' said the old lady to her slave. The
slave went out and, in an instant, returned with a woman
dressed in a clean blue cotton coat and trousers. Wang Lung
looked at her once and then turned away. His heart was
beating very fast. This woman was to be his wife.

satin, a silk cloth which is smooth and shines on one side.
opium, a substance made from the seeds of the poppy flower used to
    cause sleep and relieve pain.

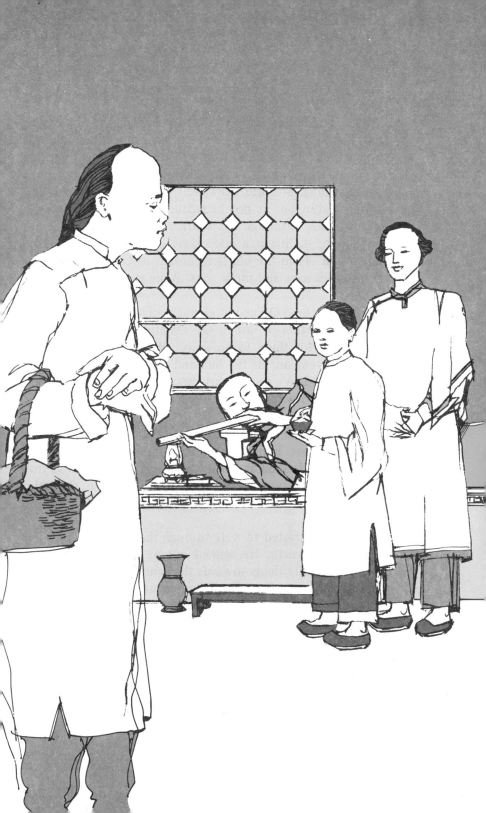

'Are you ready?' the old lady asked O-Lan.

'Ready,' she replied.

'Stand beside her while I talk to you,' said the old lady to Wang Lung. 'This woman came to our house when she was
5 ten years old. She is now twenty years old. I bought her in a year of bad crops and hunger when her parents came south from Shantung. She will work well for you in the fields and carrying water. She is not beautiful but you do not need a beautiful wife. Although she is rather slow and stupid she has
10 a good temper. She is a good slave and I hope you will be kind to her.' Then the old lady turned to O-Lan. 'Obey him and give him sons and more sons. Bring the first child to see me.'

Wang Lung and O-Lan stood and hesitated. Wang Lung did
15 not know whether or not to say something. But the old lady was anxious for them to go away. 'Well, go will you?' she said. They went out of the hall and the gatekeeper followed them with O-Lan's box on his shoulder. When they reached the small room where Wang Lung had waited, he put the box
20 down and disappeared.

Then Wang Lung looked closely at O-Lan for the first time. She had a square, honest face, a wide mouth and small, black eyes. Her face looked as if she was always silent. It was true that she was not at all beautiful but neither was she ugly.
25 Then he noticed the gold-washed earrings in her ears and he was pleased.

Wang Lung started to walk through the courts to go to the temple of the earth. He walked out of the great gates and then through the fields towards the temple. O-Lan followed
30 him and they came to a small temple made of grey bricks. A long time ago an artist had painted hills and bamboos on the white walls but the rain had washed away most of the painting. Inside the temple sat the god and goddess of the earth dressed in paper robes of red and gold.
35 In the basket Wang Lung had sticks of incense*. He took

*_incense_, a substance which gives a sweet smell when it is burned.

these out and put them in front of the god and goddess. He lit them and he and O-Lan stood and watched them burn. When the ash grew heavy, O-Lan pushed it away with her finger and then looked in fear at Wang Lung. She was afraid that she had done something wrong but Wang Lung liked her *5* pushing the ash from the incense. He thought it showed that the sticks belonged to them both now they were man and wife. For a long time they stood together in silence until the incense was all burnt.

Just as the sun was sinking, they walked home. When they *10* got to the house, Wang Lung's old father was standing by the door. He did not look at O-Lan or speak to her because that would not be proper. Instead he pretended to be very interested in the clouds. Then he saw the basket of food. 'You have spent a lot of money,' he said to his son. *15*

'There will be guests tonight,' replied Wang Lung.

'There is no end to the money you spend,' said his father, but secretly he was pleased that his son had invited guests.

Wang Lung took the food out of the basket and turned to O-Lan. 'Here is pork and beef and fish. There are seven peo- *20* ple for supper. Can you prepare food?'

'I have been a kitchen slave since I went to the House of Hwang,' replied O-Lan. 'There was meat at every meal in that house.' So she cooked the food and the guests ate the dishes and praised them very much. Wang Lung thought he had *25* never tasted such good food and he was very proud of his new wife.

3 A Child

Wang Lung's life seemed full of luxury the next morning. He woke up and watched O-Lan getting dressed and lay in bed a little longer. Then he heard his old father's dry cough. 'Take a bowl of hot water to my father,' he said to his wife.

5   'Shall I put tea with the water?' she asked.

Wang Lung wanted to say yes because he did not want O-Lan to think they were beggars. But he knew his father would not like her to give him tea the very first morning she was there. He would think it was very wasteful, so he said,

10   'Tea? No, it makes my father's cough worse.'

Then he lay for a while in his warm bed while O-Lan heated the water and made the fire. She brought him a bowl of tea. At once she was afraid that she had done something wrong.

15   'I took no tea to the old one,' she said. 'I did as you said. But to you . . .'

Wang Lung saw that she was afraid and he answered before she had finished speaking. 'I like it. I like it.' Then he drank the tea with much pleasure.

20   During the next months it seemed to Wang Lung that he just watched O-Lan while she worked. This wasn't really true because he, too, worked very hard in the fields. But it did not seem like hard work because he could come home and rest in the evening and did not have to make his own supper

25   when he was tired. When he got home, everything was ready for him and he could come in and sit at the table and eat at once.

When Wang Lung was in the fields, O-Lan worked hard. She cleaned the house and made the food. When she had

30   done this, she went outside and collected grass and leaves for the fire. This pleased Wang Lung because he did not have to buy wood for the fire. She did not rest at all until she had fed

the ox* in the evening.

She also mended their clothes and blankets. She did these things until everything was mended and the three rooms seemed very clean and almost like those of a rich man. But she never spoke very much and only talked when she needed *5* to ask Wang Lung about the house. Sometimes he wondered why this was but he never asked her. It should be enough, he thought, that she did her duty. But, at other times, he wished she would tell him about her life in the great House of Hwang. Then he would feel ashamed about his interest. She *10* was, after all, only a woman.

But, after a time, there was not enough for O-Lan to do all day in the small house. She was used to being a slave and working hard for long hours and did not like to do nothing. So, one day, she took a hoe* and went into the fields. *15*

'There is nothing for me to do in your house until night,' she said to Wang Lung and started to work beside him. They worked all day and turned over the rich, brown earth but they did not speak to each other very much.

When the sun went down, O-Lan turned to Wang Lung and *20* said, 'I am going to have a child.'

'Stop working now,' said Wang Lung. 'Come, we will go and tell my father.' They went home and told the old man, who was very happy about the thought of a grandson in his house. *25*

O-Lan made many plans for her child. 'I will take the child to the House of Hwang to visit the Old Mistress,' she told Wang Lung. 'I shall buy a red coat and red trousers for him. And on his head I will put a hat, with a small Buddha on it, and tiger shoes on his feet. I will wear new shoes, too, and a *30* new black coat, and I will show my child to everyone in the House of Hwang.'

Wang Lung was very surprised to hear her say all this because he had never heard her say so much before.

ox, a kind of cow often used to pull a cart or plough.
hoe, a tool for loosening the earth.

'I suppose you will need some money,' he said.

'Perhaps you could give me three silver pieces,' O-Lan replied. 'I know it is a lot of money but I will not waste it.'

Wang Lung took the money out of his belt. He put three
5 silver pieces on the table and then hesitated a little. Then he took a fourth piece out of the belt which he had been keeping for a long time.

'Take this piece also,' he said. 'It is our first child and his coat should be made of silk.'

10 O-Lan did not speak or move for a few minutes. She just stood and looked at the money. Then she said in a whisper, 'It is the first time I have ever had silver money in my hand.' Suddenly, she took it and hurried into the bedroom.

O-Lan had her child and it was a boy. When Wang Lung
15 heard his son's cries, he said to himself, 'Now, I suppose there will be no peace in this house.' But he was secretly very proud and happy. He went to O-Lan and said, 'Tomorrow I will go into the city and buy some red sugar for you to drink with hot water. We shall also have a big basket of eggs and
20 colour them red for our neighbours. Then everyone in the village will know that I have had a son.'

4 Good Fortune

The next day O-Lan got up and prepared food for them but she did not go to the fields with Wang Lung. He worked alone until noon. Then he dressed himself in his blue coat and went into the town. He went to the market and bought fifty eggs and some red paper to boil in water to make the 5 eggs red. Then he went to a shop that sold sweets and bought some red sugar. The man who owned the shop turned to him.

'Is it perhaps for the mother of a new child?' he asked.

'My first son,' replied Wang Lung with great pride.

'Good luck, then,' said the old man. 10

Although the man said this to many people every week, Wang Lung thought it was special. He bowed and bowed again as he left the shop and he felt he was the most fortunate man in the world. He thought of this happily at first, but then he was a little afraid. It was not good to be too 15 lucky. There were bad ghosts who were jealous of the happiness of men, especially of poor men. He must be careful. He went and bought four sticks of incense, one for each person in his house, and walked to the little temple of the earth gods. He put the sticks in the ashes of those he had burned 20 with O-Lan and felt comforted. The god and goddess would protect him and his family.

Very soon, O-Lan returned to the fields. The harvests were over now, so they beat the grain and planted the fields with seed for the winter crops. They worked at this all day and 25 their son lay asleep on the ground beside them.

Winter came but they were ready for it. The harvests had been the best Wang Lung had ever known and the small house was so full of grain and food that it was almost bursting. There were dried onions and garlic hanging from the roof and 30 great jars of wheat and rice. Most of this food would be sold later but there was no hurry. Wang Lung did not waste his

money. He was careful and did not need to sell his food until the prices were good. He liked to save it until the snow came at New Year when people would pay well for food. Many farmers had to sell their grain as soon as the harvest was over
5 because they had wasted their money and had none left. Wang Lung's uncle often had to sell his crops before they were even ripe. Sometimes he even sold it standing in the field so that he did not have the work of cutting it. His uncle's wife wasted much money on expensive food and new
10 clothes and shoes so there was never anything hanging in Wang Lung's uncle's house. But, this year, in Wang Lung's house, there was even a leg of pork hanging from the roof. Wang Lung had bought this from his neighbour Ching who had killed a sick pig. The pig had not grown thin and the leg
15 was a good, large one. O-Lan had put salt on it and put it to dry. Beside the leg of pork, there were two of their own chickens also covered with salt.

In the middle of all this plenty, they sat in the house and kept warm when the cold, winter winds came. Soon the child
20 could almost sit on his own. They had a feast on his month day, and everyone who came to the house praised the fat, handsome child. Soon the leaves fell from the trees and only the bamboo leaves remained. The dry wind continued and Wang Lung prayed for rain. Without rain, the wheat seed he
25 had planted could not grow.

At last the rain came and the air seemed warm and quiet. They all sat happily in the house watching the rain fall and sink into the dry earth. The child watched the rain and stretched out his hands to try to catch the silver lines that
30 ran down the window. They laughed with him and the old man sat beside him on the floor and said, 'There is not another child like this one in a dozen villages. My brother's children noticed nothing properly before they could walk. This is a very clever child.' And in the fields the wheat seed
35 grew and its green sticks appeared above the wet, brown earth.

At a time like this all the farmers went to visit each other because they felt that heaven had been kind to them and sent rain to their fields. In the morning they gathered at one of their houses and drank tea together. The women stayed at home and mended clothes and made shoes, and thought about the New Year.   5

But Wang Lung did not go and visit the other farmers. There was no other house in the village that was so full of warmth and good grain as his. He did not want the other farmers to try to borrow money from him. He thought if they saw how much he had they would want him to share it   10 with them. And Wang Lung wanted to keep his good crops and sell them just before the New Year so that they could have a good feast. So Wang Lung and O-Lan stayed at home and Wang Lung mended the farm tools and O-Lan mended the house tools. If there was a leak in a jar, she did not throw   15 it away but mended it with earth and water and heated it until it was like new.

It had been a good year for the crops and Wang Lung had saved some extra money. After they had worked out how much they needed for themselves, there was still some left.   20 But Wang Lung did not want anyone except O-Lan to know about this money so they talked together and tried to decide where to hide it. At last, O-Lan dug a small hole in the wall behind the bed. Wang Lung put his silver in this hole and O-Lan covered it with a piece of earth. It looked as though   25 there was nothing there, but Wang Lung and O-Lan knew about their secret treasure.

5 The New Year

The New Year came nearer and there were many preparations in the houses in the village. Wang Lung went into the town and bought candles and squares of red paper. He put the red paper on his plough and his tools, and on the doors of his
5 house, to bring him good luck. Then he bought red paper to make into dresses for the earth gods. The old man made the dresses very carefully and Wang Lung took them to the temple and put them on the god and goddess. Then he burned some incense in front of them. In his own house, he put two
10 red candles under the picture of the earth god to burn on the evening before the New Year.

Again, Wang Lung went into the town and, this time, he bought pork fat and white sugar. O-Lan took the fat and the sugar and some rice flour and made cakes for the New Year.
15 These were rich moon cakes like those which the rich people ate each year in the great House of Hwang. She laid the cakes out on the table and Wang Lung saw them and was very proud. There was no other woman in the village who could make cakes like these which the rich ate at their feasts. In
20 some of the cakes, O-Lan put little red berries and other kinds of fruit in the shapes of flowers and patterns.

'It is a pity to eat these,' said Wang Lung. And the old man walked around the table looking at the pretty cakes like a child.

25 'Call my brother and his children,' he said. 'Let them come and see the cakes.'

But Wang Lung did not think this was a good idea. His uncle was not as wealthy as he was and he could not ask them to look at the cakes. They were hungry and would want to
30 eat them. So he said, 'No, it is bad luck to look at the cakes before the New Year.'

O-Lan then said, 'These cakes are not for us to eat. Our

guests may perhaps taste one or two of the plain ones but the others are for the Old Mistress at the House of Hwang. On the second day of the New Year, I shall take our child to the great house and carry the cakes as a gift.'

Then the cakes seemed more important and Wang Lung *5* was pleased that O-Lan was going to take them to the great house in the town. The Old Mistress would see then how successful Wang Lung was and how fortunate he had been in the past year. Everything else at New Year seemed less important to Wang Lung than this visit. Even when his relatives *10* came to the house, he only thought of the House of Hwang.

On the second day of the New Year, they got up very early in the morning. O-Lan dressed their son in his red coat and tiger shoes and the hat with the Buddha. Then Wang Lung dressed in his new black robe and O-Lan put on her new coat *15* and tied her hair with a silver pin. Then they set out carrying their son and the cakes across the fields.

At the great gate of the House of Hwang, Wang Lung was given a reward for all his hard work. This time, the gatekeeper looked at him with much respect. 'Ah, Wang the farmer,' he *20* said, 'this time there are three of you instead of only one.' Then he noticed their new clothes, 'I see you have had very good luck in the past year.'

Wang Lung answered carelessly like a man who is speaking to a poor man. 'Yes, yes, good harvests — good harvests.' *25*

The gatekeeper turned to Wang Lung, 'Please sir, come inside my poor room while I take your wife and son to the Old Mistress.' Wang Lung stood and watched them walk across the court and then he went into the little room where the gatekeeper sat. Wang Lung sat in the place of honour and *30* the man's wife gave him a bowl of tea.

It seemed a very long time until the gatekeeper returned with O-Lan and the child. Wang Lung looked carefully at his wife's face to try and see if she was happy. He saw that she looked contented and they left the gatekeeper and his wife *35* and walked out of the gates. 'Well?' he asked because he wanted to hear what had happened inside the great house.

O-Lan came a little closer to him and whispered softly, 'I believe that they are almost poor in the great house now.'

'What do you mean?' asked Wang Lung. 'The Ancient Mistress was wearing the same coat this year as last New Year,' replied O-Lan. 'I have never seen this happen before. And the slaves did not have new coats. There was not even one slave with a coat like mine. There was no child as beautiful as our son in the House of Hwang and none of the children was so finely dressed.'

A smile spread slowly across O-Lan's face and Wang Lung felt very glad. How well he had done! How well he had done! He had a good wife and a handsome son and the harvests had been good. But then he remembered the evil ghosts who did not like men to be too successful. He hid the child under his coat and pretended that it was a girl child.

'Did you ask why they are so poor?' asked Wang Lung.

'I only talked to the cook for a minute,' replied O-Lan. 'But she says that the five young lords all spend very much money in foreign places. They send women home, too, and that is very expensive. And the third daughter is to be married in the spring and they have to pay for a large wedding and new clothes for her.'

Then O-Lan paused and continued after a few minutes, 'They must be almost poor now because the Old Mistress told me they wanted to sell some land. They want especially to sell the land to the south of the house, just outside the city wall. They have always planted rice there and it is good land. Because it is near the moat, there is plenty of water.'

'Sell their land!' said Wang Lung. 'They must certainly need money very much.' Then he was silent and thought for a while. Suddenly, he had an idea and he hit the side of his head with his hand. 'Why haven't I thought of it before?' He said to O-Lan. 'I will buy the land.'

They looked at each other in great surprise.

'I will buy it,' said Wang Lung. 'I will buy it from the House of Hwang.'

'But it is too far away from our house,' said O-Lan in a

worried voice. 'We would have to walk for half the morning
to get to it.'

'I will buy it anyway,' replied Wang Lung.

'It is a good thing to buy land,' said O-Lan. 'It is better
5 than keeping the money in a mud wall. But why don't you
buy some of your uncle's land? I know he wants to sell that
piece of land near to our field in the west.'

'That land!' cried Wang Lung. 'I will not buy my uncle's
land. He has not looked after it properly. It would not grow
10 good crops for me. I will buy Hwang's land.'

He said 'Hwang's land' just as if he was speaking about the
land of a neighbour. He would be as good as those rich, wasteful people in the great House of Hwang. He would buy their
land. Then Wang Lung began to imagine how he would go to
15 the Old Lord's house with silver in his hand and say, 'Look at
this money. I have it here in my hand. What is the fair price
for your land? Sell it to me. I am as good as any other man.'

Then O-Lan, who had been a slave in the kitchen, stopped
worrying. She was proud to be married to a man who was
20 going to own Hwang's land – land which had belonged to
Hwang's family for hundreds of years. She turned to Wang
Lung. 'Let the land be bought. Rice land is good and it is
near the moat. It will be easy to carry water to it. It is a good
idea.'

6 Hwang's Land

Wang Lung bought the piece of land near the moat and it seemed at first that it changed his whole life. He felt a little sad when he gave his silver for the land. He knew the land would need a lot of hard work and now he had no more money hidden in the hole in the mud wall. Also, when he had 5 gone to buy the land, he was a little disappointed. The occasion had not been as splendid as he had hoped.

One morning he had gone to the great house just before noon to see the Old Lord. But the Old Lord was still asleep. Wang Lung said to the gatekeeper, 'Tell him that I have im- 10 portant business with him. Tell him it is about money.'

But the man had replied, 'All the money in the world would not make me wake the Old Lord. Silver will not wake him up. He has always had plenty of that.'

In the end, the business was done between Wang Lung and 15 the Old Lord's manager who was a wicked and greedy man.

But the land was his now and this made Wang Lung feel a little happier. One grey day, he set out to look at it. No one knew yet that he had bought Hwang's land and he went to see it alone. It was a long square of heavy, black clay beside 20 the moat. It was three hundred paces* in length and one hundred and twenty across. There were four stones at the corners of the land to show that this was Hwang's land. Wang Lung thought he would change that. He would pull up the stones and put his own name there. He would not do it this 25 year, though, because he did not want people to know how much money he had. He looked at the piece of land and thought to himself, 'This land means nothing to the people in the House of Hwang. But to me it is very precious.' Then he became angry that a small piece of land was so important to 30

*pace, the distance covered by the foot in one step.

him. He became determined that he would buy more and
more land. He decided that he would once more fill the hole
in the wall with silver. He thought that Hwang's land was a
sign that he would be really rich one day.

5   Spring came and brought winds and clouds of rain and
Wang Lung began to work very hard on his land. The old man
now looked after the child and O-Lan worked with Wang
Lung from morning until night. Then, one day, she had
another child. It was another boy and all the family was very
10   glad. The harvests were good and now the people in the
village knew that Wang Lung had bought Hwang's land.

Wang Lung felt that everything was good but then his
uncle began to make trouble for him. He had known for a
long time that this might happen. His uncle was his father's
15   younger brother and he thought it was Wang Lung's duty to
look after him and give him money. When Wang Lung was
poor, his uncle had to work to make money for himself, his
wife and his seven children. But his uncle did not like work
and only did just enough to feed them. Now he was jealous
20   of Wang Lung's good fortune.

One day Wang Lung went to his uncle's house to talk to
his aunt. 'It is a disgrace to our family that your eldest
daughter is not yet married,' Wang Lung said to her. 'She still
runs around the village like a young girl. It is time she was
25   married.'

'Yes,' replied Wang Lung's aunt. 'But who will pay for the
wedding and her dowry*? You are rich and have much land
and plenty of spare money. You can afford to buy more and
more land from the great families in the town. But your
30   uncle is not a fortunate man like you. He has always suffered
bad luck. It is not his fault but the will of heaven. However
hard he works he cannot produce good crops. The seed dies
in the ground and only weeds grow in his land.'

After she had said this, she started to cry very loudly and
35   pulled her long hair and screamed, 'You do not know what it

*dowry, property and/or money brought by a bride to her husband.

is like to have bad luck. Other men's fields produce good crops but ours do not. Other men's houses remain strong for years and years while ours shakes as if the walls would crack. Other women have sons, but I do not.'

Wang Lung was calm while she shouted. 'I still think your daughter should be married,' he said. Then he went away from his uncle's house. His lazy relatives made him angry. He wanted to buy more land from the House of Hwang this year and then more and more land. He even thought of building a new room on to his house. But he could not forget the disgrace of his uncle's family.

The next day, Wang Lung's uncle came to the field where he was working. He did not look clean and his clothes were not properly fastened. He stood near to Wang Lung but did not say anything. At last Wang Lung turned to him. 'I am sorry to make you wait, my uncle,' he said. 'But I have to sow these seeds. I am sure you have done all your work but I am a slow farmer.'

Wang Lung's uncle understood that these words were meant to hurt him but he replied, 'I am a man who has bad luck. This year I planted beans but only one plant grew. If we are to eat beans this year, I shall have to buy them.'

Wang Lung tried not to feel sorry about his uncle's bad luck. He knew that he had come to ask for money. He went on working while his uncle continued, 'My wife has told me you are interested in my daughter. What you say is true. She should be married. I do not want to disgrace our family. If I had your good luck and extra money, I would share it with you. I would help you find husbands for your daughters and good jobs for your sons. I would also be glad to repair your house and give you food.'

Wang Lung answered him, 'You know I am not rich. I have five people to feed in my house and my old father does not work. Soon my wife will have another child.'

'But you are rich! You are rich!' cried the uncle. 'You have bought land from the great house. There is no other man in the village who has enough money to buy such land.'

These words made Wang Lung very angry. He shouted at his uncle, 'If I have bought land with silver, it is because I have worked very hard for the money. My wife also works hard. We are not like some people who sit in a dirty house
5   talking all the time and playing games for money.'

When he heard this, Wang Lung's uncle became very red in the face. He rushed towards his nephew and hit him hard on both cheeks. 'You cannot speak to me like that,' he said. 'I am your uncle, your father's brother. You should speak to
10   me with respect. I will tell the whole village that you have insulted me.'

Now this made Wang Lung feel very foolish and worried. He did not want everyone in the village to know he had quarrelled with his uncle.

15   'What do you want me to do then?' he asked.

Immediately, his uncle's face changed and his anger went away. He smiled and put his hand on Wang Lung's arm in a very friendly way. 'Ah, you are a good boy. You are like a son to me. Please give me a little silver, my son. Give some
20   silver to your old uncle. Ten pieces would be enough. Then I can begin to arrange my daughter's wedding. You are quite right. It is time she was married.'

Wang Lung picked up his hoe and threw it on to the ground. 'Come to my house,' he said. 'I do not carry silver on
25   me like a prince,' Then he started to walk towards his house without saying any more to his uncle. He walked into the house and went to the bedroom where the silver was hidden. His wife was there with a new baby. This time the child was a girl. 'A bad omen,' thought Wang Lung. A girl was the cause
30   of all the trouble in his uncle's house and now there was a girl child in his own house.

He went to the hole in the wall and took out the silver.

'Why are you doing that?' O-Lan asked suddenly.

'I must lend it to my uncle. It is my duty.'

35   'Do not say lend,' replied O-Lan. 'There is no lending in your uncle's house. He will not pay it back to you. You know that. You are giving it to him.'

'Yes, I know,' said Wang Lung. 'But he is my uncle and he needs money. I have no choice.'

Then he walked out of the room and quickly gave the money to his uncle. As soon as he had done this, he walked back to the fields and went on working. He thought about the silver and put all his anger into the earth as he worked. It was almost dark when he stopped working. Suddenly, he was very sad. Now, he could not buy more land from the House of Hwang because he had given the money to his uncle. Just then, a flock of black crows flew above him like a black cloud. They flew into the trees above Wang Lung's house and then in circles above his head. At last they flew away into the dark sky.

It was another evil omen.

7 No Rain

It seemed to Wang Lung that now everything would go badly for his family. The rain, which the crops needed, did not come at the usual time. Day after day, a brilliant sun shone and there was not a single cloud in the sky. At night, the stars 5 shone with a golden light and a cruel beauty.

The fields became dry and the earth cracked even though Wang Lung looked after them very carefully. The young wheat stopped growing and, at last, turned yellow and died in the hot sun. Wang Lung carried water to the fields each day 10 but it was no good. Then the water in the pond dried up and even the water in the well sank so low that O-Lan said to him, 'If the children must drink and the old man must have hot water, then the plants will have to die.'

'But if the plants do not grow,' said Wang Lung, 'we will 15 have no food. We will die of hunger.'

The only crops which lived were those in the land by the moat. This was because Wang Lung stopped going to the other fields and only put water on Hwang's land. This year, for the first time in his life, he sold his crops as soon as the 20 grain was ready. When he had the silver in his hand, he felt a little happier and he hurried to the House of Hwang to buy more land.

Now Wang Lung had heard that it had been a very hard year for the great house. The Old Mistress had not been given 25 enough opium and the young lords had been angry because there was not enough money for them to spend. When the manager, therefore, saw Wang Lung and his money, he took the silver eagerly and gave Wang Lung a big field of good land. This field was almost twice as large as the piece by the 30 moat and Wang Lung told no one he had bought it.

Several months passed and there was still no rain. As Autumn came nearer, small clouds gathered in the sky and men watched them anxiously. But, before there were enough clouds to make rain, a dry wind came and blew them away.

From his fields Wang Lung managed to collect a few beans and a very little grain. He wasted nothing but there was very little food even though he was so careful. Everyone in the   *5* village was hungry and soon there was almost no food left. When there was no rice and no wheat, the old man said to his son, 'Now, we will have to eat the ox.'

This made Wang Lung very miserable because the ox was his companion in the fields and he had worked for a long   *10* time with this ox. So he said, 'How can we eat the ox? We cannot plough the fields if we do not have an ox.'

But the old man replied, 'Well, it is either your life or the ox's. If we do not eat the ox, we will die. It is easier to buy another ox than to buy a man's life.'   *15*

Wang Lung knew this was true but he could not kill the animal. Many days passed and the children cried because they were hungry and nothing comforted them. At last, Wang Lung turned to O-Lan and said, 'Let the animal be killed. But I cannot do it myself. Do not ask me to kill it.' Then he went   *20* into the room where he slept and covered his head with a blanket so that he could not hear the ox's screams.

O-Lan killed the ox and cut up the meat and made soup. At first, Wang Lung could not eat the meat and only drank a very little of the soup. Then O-Lan said to him, 'It was only   *25* an old ox. Eat some of the meat. One day we will buy another ox which will be much better than this one.' These kind words comforted Wang Lung and he ate some of the meat, and all his family ate, and they felt better. But it seemed that the meat was soon finished and again there was no more food.   *30*

At first, when the rain did not come, the farmers were angry with Wang Lung. They thought that he had a lot of silver hidden in his house and they had nothing. They were sure, too, that he had good stores of food as well as silver. One day Wang Lung's uncle came to the house to ask for   *35* food for himself, his wife and seven children. Wang Lung gave him a small heap of beans and a little corn but his uncle thought this was not enough. He came again to the house and, this time, Wang Lung sent him away with nothing. After this, his uncle hated Wang Lung and whispered bad things about his nephew to the other farmers.

5   'Wang Lung,' he said, 'has plenty of food and silver in his house but he will not share it with us. He will not even give some to his own family.'

One by one, each family in the village finished their food and the street was full of hungry people and crying children.

10   The cold winter winds came and Wang Lung's uncle walked in the streets like a hungry dog. He talked to everyone he met and said, 'There is a man whose children are still fat. He still has food.' So one night the men took poles and went in a group to Wang Lung's house and banged on his door. Wang

15   Lung opened the door to his neighbours, and they rushed in and searched every corner of his house for food. But they only found a few beans and a little corn because that was all Wang Lung had. Then they tried to take away all the furniture but O-Lan prevented them. 'Do not take that,' she said.

20   'It is not yet time to take away our table and benches. You have taken all our food. But you have not yet sold your own furniture from your houses. It is not fair to take ours. Come with me to the fields and we will collect grass for our children to eat.'

25   Then they all went away and Wang Lung stood and looked at his land. He felt very miserable and, for a moment, he was very afraid. Then he said to himself, 'They have taken my food. But they cannot take away my land. I have put all my work into that land and they cannot take it away from me.

30   If I had silver, they would steal it. I have no silver so they cannot take it. I only have the land.'

Although he still had the land, Wang Lung knew that he must do something. They could not stay in the village and die of hunger. He was determined to live and to buy more land.

35   But sometimes he felt very angry and shouted at the cruel gods. Once he even went and spat at the earth gods in the little temple. There were no sticks of incense in front of the

gods now and their paper clothes were old and torn. The farmers thought the gods were cruel and would not go to the temple in a year of bad harvests. But the gods looked as if they did not care. Wang Lung went home and lay on his bed.

Wang Lung and his family now did not get up in the 5 morning. There was no work for them to do and they were too weak to do anything. Sometimes the two boys sat in the sun for a little while but the girl child just lay wrapped in an old blanket and hardly ever moved. The old man was the happiest of them all because he was given any food that they 10 had.

One day their neighbour Ching came to their house and told them what was happening in the town. 'The people there are eating dogs,' he said. 'In our village we have eaten the grass and the bark* of the trees. What is there for us to eat 15 now? In the village some people are even eating human flesh. The people say your uncle is doing this. He and his wife must be eating human flesh because we know they have no food.'

When Wang Lung heard this, he was very frightened. He got up from his chair quickly. 'We will leave this place,' he 20 said. 'We will go south rather than die here.'

The next morning, as the sun was rising, Wang Lung stood and thought about their long journey. Perhaps he was stupid? How could they drag their bodies for a hundred miles or more? Perhaps there wasn't any food in the south? How 25 could he know? Maybe it would be more sensible to stay where they were?

As he was thinking, his uncle walked up to the house. There were three other men with him whom Wang Lung did not recognize. Wang Lung's uncle was thin but he did not 30 look like a very hungry man.

'What have you eaten? How have you managed to eat?' Wang Lung asked. His uncle opened his eyes very wide and raised his hands up towards the sky.

'We have nothing,' he said. 'My wife, who used to be big 35

---

*bark, the outside part of a tree.

and fat, is now all skin and bones. Three of our children have died of hunger.'

'But you have eaten something,' said Wang Lung in a dull voice.

5 'I have only thought of you and your father,' said his uncle quickly, 'and now I have come to prove it to you. As soon as I could I borrowed some food from these three good men. Because they gave me food, I promised I would help them buy some land. Then I thought at once of your good land,
10 the land of my brother's son. They have come with me to buy your land and to give you money.'

Wang Lung did not move. He did not even look straight at the three men for a few minutes. Then he lifted his eyes and saw that they were men from the town. They were dressed in
15 dirty robes of silk and their hands were soft. Their finger-nails were long and they did not look hungry. Suddenly, Wang Lung hated these men.

'I will not sell my land,' he said.

At that moment, the younger of his sons came out of the
20 house on his hands and knees. He had so little strength he could not even walk. They all looked at the child and Wang Lung began to cry miserable tears.

'What is your price?'

'We will give you one hundred pence,' they replied.

25 'But that is taking the land as if it was a gift,' said Wang Lung. 'When I buy land, I pay twenty times that. No, I will never sell my land.'

Just then, O-Lan came out of the house and said, 'No, we will not sell the land. But we will sell our table, beds, blan-
30 kets and four benches.' And the men gave her two silver pieces and took the furniture away with them.

Then O-Lan turned to Wang Lung and said, 'Let us go now while we have this money and before we have to sell the roof of our house.'

35 'Yes,' replied Wang Lung sadly, 'we will go.'

8 Journey to the South

When they had decided to go, there was nothing left to do
except shut the door of their house and fasten the bolts.
They had all their clothes on them so there was not much for
them to carry. O-Lan gave a rice bowl and a pair of chopsticks to each of the boys and they all started to walk across   *5*
the fields. At first, Wang Lung held the girl child, but then he
gave her to O-Lan and carried his old father who could hardly
walk. A cold wind blew and blew and they walked without
speaking past the little temple. The two boys cried because
they were so cold and hungry. Wang Lung tried hard to com-   *10*
fort them and said, 'You are two big men and you are travellers to the south. There is warmth there and food every day.
When we get there, you will have white rice and as much to
eat as you want.'

At last they reached the town and walked towards the   *15*
House of Hwang but there was no one outside the house and
they walked on. When they had walked through the main
part of the town, they saw a crowd of people all walking
slowly. Wang Lung stopped and asked one of them where
they were all going. The man replied, 'We are hungry people   *20*
and we are going to the south. We are going to get on the
train which will take us away from this place. It leaves from
that house over there. There are wagons for poor people like
us which cost only a small silver piece.'

Trains! In the past, Wang Lung had heard men in the town   *25*
talking about these vehicles which were tied to each other
with chains and pulled by a machine. And the machine blew
water and fire from its mouth like a dragon. He had often
wished to go and see one of these strange monsters, but he
had never done so. Now he turned to O-Lan and said, 'Shall   *30*
we also go on this train?'

Then they both looked at the old man and the children

and saw how tired they were.

'Come on,' said Wang Lung. 'We will go and get on to this train and sit all the way to the south.'

Wang Lung gave an officer, who collected money for the train, two pieces of silver for a journey of one hundred miles. The officer gave him back some copper pieces and, with these, he bought four small loaves of bread and a bowl of soft rice. But he did not spend all the copper pieces. He kept some of them to buy mats to build a shed for them when they reached the south.

Inside the train, there were men and women who went to the south every year. They travelled to the rich cities of the south to work and to live as beggars. If they worked and then begged for food, they managed to save the price of food. Wang Lung listened to the advice of one of the men, 'First,' he said, 'you must buy six mats. These should cost two pence each and you must not pay more than that. Then you must make the mats into a shed. When you have done this, you should cover yourself with mud and go out into the streets as a beggar. It is also a good idea to have something to eat first. These people in the south have so much rice that there are big public kitchens where a bowl of white rice soup costs only a penny. Then, when you have eaten, you can beg without feeling hungry. With the money you get, you can buy cabbage and garlic.'

Now Wang Lung had never in his life been a beggar and the thought of begging made him feel very ashamed. He turned away and counted his money. There was enough for the six mats and for a penny bowl of rice soup each and three pence over. He felt a little comforted. Perhaps they really could begin a new life in the south. But he still did not like the thought of earning his food as a beggar.

'Is there no work for a man?'

One of the travellers spat on the floor. 'Oh, work,' he said scornfully. 'You can pull a rich man in a rickshaw*, if you

*rickshaw, a vehicle with two wheels which carries one or two passengers and which is pulled by a man.

like. You can run until you sweat and freeze while you wait
for a customer. But it is much better to be a beggar.'
     But Wang Lung was glad to hear that there was some work
and he made a plan. When the train arrived, he put the old
man beside the long, grey wall of a house, with the children.   5
Then he told O-Lan to stay with them and look after them
while he went to buy the mats. As he walked, he asked
people which way to go. At first, he could not understand
what they said because their voices were different from
people's in the north. But at last he found a shop which sold   10
mats and he bought six and returned to his family. The children did not like being in a strange place and were afraid, but
the old man looked at everything with great interest. 'Look,'
he said, 'how fat and oily these people are. See how pale their
skins are. They must surely eat pork every day.' But none of   15
the people who walked past looked at Wang Lung and his
family.
     O-Lan made a small hut out of the mats against the wall of
the house. There were many other huts in this place where
poor people lived who earned their money pulling rickshaws   20
or begging.
     'Now,' said Wang Lung, 'we will go the public kitchen and
find some food.'
     As they left their hut, they saw many people carrying
empty rice bowls so they followed them until they reached   25
the big kitchen for the poor. It was a large shed made out of
mats and inside there were hundreds of people with empty
bowls. They were all fighting like animals for the food, but,
at last, Wang Lung and his family filled their bowls. Wang
Lung stood outside the kitchen eating his food. When there   30
was just a little left in the bowl, he said to O-Lan, 'I will take
this home and eat it this evening.'
     But a guard, who was standing nearby, stopped him. 'You
must not take it away,' he said. 'You are allowed only to take
away what you have eaten. We have to make this rule or   35
some mean people take the food and give it to their pigs.'
     Wang Lung was very surprised to hear that there were

people who did this, and then he asked who gave the food for the poor.

'The rich people in the town,' replied the guard. 'They give food for the poor so that they will get praise in heaven or as a
5   good deed which will bring them good luck. Some people give the food so that other men will speak well of them.' Wang Lung wanted to ask the man more questions, but the guard was tired of speaking to him and turned away. The children and the old man were very tired and they all went
10 back to the hut. There they all slept well until the morning. It was the first time since the summer that they had gone to sleep full of food.

9 Foreigners

The next morning, they had to get some more money. They spent the last copper coin on rice soup and Wang Lung looked at O-Lan and wondered what they should do. 'I and the children will beg,' said O-Lan, 'and the old man, too. His grey hairs will make people feel sorry for us and they will _5_ give us money.'

And she called the two boys and said to them, 'Each of you take your rice bowls and hold them like this . . . ' She took an empty bowl and held it out in front of her and cried in a miserable voice, 'Have a good heart, kind sir, kind lady. _10_ Earn praise in heaven. Give a copper coin to feed a hungry child.'

The boys and Wang Lung looked at her. Wang Lung could not believe it. How did she know how to cry like a beggar? There was so much about O-Lan that he did not know. O-Lan _15_ saw what he was thinking and said, 'I learned how to do it when I was a child. It was in a year of hunger like this one that I was sold as a slave to the House of Hwang.'

The old man and the boys went out to beg and O-Lan went with them carrying the girl child in her arms. Each time _20_ someone passed them, O-Lan held out her bowl in front of her and said, 'Unless you give us some coins, dear sir, dear lady, we will die of hunger. This child will die.'

But the boys did not like doing this and felt ashamed. This made O-Lan very angry and she hit their faces until they _25_ began to cry. 'There!' she said. 'That will stop you laughing. Now, go and beg.'

Wang Lung went into the streets and looked for a place where he could hire* a rickshaw. At last, he managed to hire one for a day which he could pay for in the evening. As he _30_

---

*_to hire_, to use something in return for money.

pulled the old, wooden rickshaw behind him, he felt as if he
were an ox and he could hardly walk. But he knew he must
be able to run if he was to earn money in this way. He went
into a little, empty street and tried to get used to pulling the
5   awkward rickshaw.

Then a man, who was dressed as a teacher, came out of a nearby door and climbed into Wang Lung's rickshaw. 'Take me to the Confucian Temple,' he said and sat up very straight. Wang Lung did not know how to get to this temple and he did not dare to ask the teacher. But he asked people as he ran *5* along and, at last, he reached the temple. When the teacher got down from the rickshaw, he gave Wang Lung a small silver coin. 'Now, do not complain,' said the teacher. 'I never pay more than this.' Wang Lung did not want to complain because the silver seemed a lot of money to him. He was not *10* quite sure, though, how much it was worth and he took it to a rice shop. The man in the rice shop gave him twenty-six pence for it and Wang Lung was very pleased, but another rickshaw man turned to him. 'Only twenty-six pence,' he said. 'That is not enough. You must argue about the price *15* before you begin your journey. The only people with whom you need not argue are white foreigners. They are fools and always give silver.' The other men who pulled rickshaws all laughed at Wang Lung because he was only a farmer from the north and had not made a better bargain with the teacher. *20*

Wang Lung had one more passenger during the morning and two in the afternoon. But, in the evening, when he counted his money, he had only one penny more than the rent of the rickshaw. He was very unhappy and said to himself. 'I have worked harder than ever before, and I am very *25* tired, but I have only earned one penny.' Then he remembered his land which was waiting for him and the thought comforted him a little.

O-Lan had received five pence and the boys had got enough money to pay for the rice soup in the morning, but the old *30* man had received no coins at all. All day he had just sat and sometimes he had slept but he did not beg. And, because he was old, O-Lan could not scold him. When he saw that he had no money, he only said, 'I have ploughed the land and I have planted seed. I have fed my family and I have had a son and *35* grandsons.'

Now that Wang Lung saw that his family had food each

day, he felt a little less strange in the city. He began to get to know the places as he ran each day with his rickshaw. He learned that in the morning the women he carried in the rickshaw usually wanted to go to the market. The men usual-
5 ly wanted to go to the schools and the houses of business. But he did not know anything about these places except their names because he never went inside them.

But, although he became used to the city, he still felt like a foreigner in a new place. The language sounded different
10 from the language in the north and the people ate different foods. In his home in the north, the farmers grew rice, wheat, corn, beans and garlic. But here, they also grew many other vegetables which Wang Lung had never seen before. The people in the south laughed at Wang Lung's piece of bread
15 with good garlic inside it. When he went into a shop to buy cloth, it seemed as if the owner increased the price because of the smell of the garlic.

But one day Wang Lung learned that there were real for-eigners in this city, people who came from a different coun-
20 try. He was passing the door of a shop that sold silk and a strange creature came out. He did not know whether it was a man or a woman. It was tall and dressed in a long, black robe with the skin of a dead animal around its neck. It got into the rickshaw and asked Wang Lung to go to the Street of Bridges.
25 As Wang Lung ran, he shouted to people, 'Look at this. What is it?'

And a man replied, 'That is a foreigner, a woman from America. You are a lucky man. She will give you a lot of money.' But Wang Lung did not care about the money. He
30 was frightened of this strange woman and he ran as fast as he could until he reached the Street of Bridges.

When he stopped, the woman said, 'You should not have run so fast. You look so tired. Here are two silver pieces.' This was twice the normal fare, and, when he got home,
35 Wang Lung told O-Lan about the strange American woman.

'Yes,' said O-Lan. 'I have seen these people, too. They are the only people who put silver coins into our bowls when we are begging. They are foolish and do not know that it is proper to give copper to beggars.'

It seemed to O-Lan and Wang Lung that no one could die of hunger in this rich city. There was good food everywhere. There were great baskets of fish in the fish market and huge   *5* baskets of grain and vegetables in the other markets. And there were shops which sold all kinds of delicious food and vegetables. But, in spite of all this food, hundreds of people went each day to the public kitchen for a bowl of rice soup. Even though O-Lan begged and Wang Lung worked, they   *10* never had enough money to cook rice in their own hut every day.

One day, however, Wang Lung came home and saw that O-Lan was cooking a piece of pork. They had not had meat for a long time and he was very surprised. 'You must have   *15* been given money by a foreigner today,' he said.

O-Lan said nothing. But the younger boy cried, 'I took it. It is my meat. I stole it from the butcher* when he was not looking.'

When he heard this, Wang Lung was very angry with his   *20* younger son. 'I will not eat this meat,' he said. 'We will eat meat if we can buy it or beg for it. But we will not eat meat which we have stolen.' Then he took the meat out of the pot and threw it on to the floor and would not listen to the cries of his son. But O-Lan walked forward very quietly and   *25* picked up the meat from the floor, then she washed it and put it back into the pot.

Although Wang Lung said nothing else about the meat then, he was worried and angry. He thought that his sons were learning to be thieves in this foreign city. After the meal   *30* was finished, he took his younger son into the street and hit his head to punish him. But to himself he said, 'We must go back to the land. This town is not a good place for my family.'

butcher, a person who kills, cuts up and sells animals for food.

10 Strange News

Day after day, Wang Lung worked in this rich city and each day he noticed how poor the people in the huts were and how rich the people in the large houses were. All day men worked baking bread and cakes for the feasts of the rich, but 5 there was not enough food for them and their children. And all day men and women worked at cutting and making fur coats for the rich people to wear in the winter and soft, light furs for them to wear in the summer. But the people who made them had only enough money for a bit of coarse, 10 cotton cloth for themselves.

Wang Lung lived amongst people who worked so that the rich people could have huge feasts and splendid clothes. Sometimes he heard strange talk about a revolution when the workers would fight the rich people, but he did not under- 15 stand. The old men and women did not talk like this. It was only the young men who spoke angry words about the rich people.

At the end of one winter day, Wang Lung stood outside his hut and talked to the old man. He was full of a great desire to 20 see his land and to work in his fields. 'Shall I never see it again?' he asked sadly.

Then he heard a deep voice which said, 'You are not the only man who feels like that. There are a thousand like you in this city.' The man who had spoken walked up to Wang 25 Lung. He was the father of the family who lived in the hut next to Wang Lung's hut. During the day they did not often see him because he slept all day and worked all night pulling heavy carts.

'Well, and will it always be like this for us?' Wang Lung 30 asked.

'No,' replied the man, 'not always. There will come a time when the rich are not too rich. Something will happen which

will alter all this. The young men are talking with anger and
soon there will be changes. Have you seen inside that wall?'
He pointed to the wall where the huts stood. Wang Lung
shook his head. 'In there even the servants eat with chopsticks which are bound with silver. Even the slaves have jade   5
earrings and sew pearls on to their shoes. When the shoes
have a little piece of dirt on them, they throw them away.
They even throw away the pearls.'
    Wang Lung could not sleep that night. He kept thinking
about the rich people inside the wall. For a while, he was   10
tempted to sell his girl child as a slave there. If he did, she
would have fine clothes and plenty of food and pearls for her
shoes. But then he said to himself, 'No, I will not sell one of
my children. Even if I sold her, we would not have enough
money to go back to our home and buy an ox, a table, a bed   15
and seed to plant in the fields.'
    Spring came and everyone thought of their homes in the
country. Each day, Wang Lung saw women and children leave
the huts and go into the country to collect food from the
roads. Wang Lung went on working and he listened to the   20
men who worked with him. These men always talked about
the money which they earned and they always said the same
thing. 'If only I had the money that a rich man has . . . '
    Once Wang Lung said, 'If I had enough money, I would
buy land and grow good crops.' But they all laughed at this   25
and said, 'Here is a foolish farmer who wants to work like a
slave all his life.'
    Wang Lung went on working and did not understand what
the men in the city said and the pieces of paper that men
gave to each other. He did not know how to read and one   30
day he asked someone to explain the words on the paper to
him. There was a picture, too, on this piece of paper. It was
of a poor, dead man in old blue clothes and beside the dead
man there was a great, fat, rich man. The rich man was killing
the poor man with a knife. The man to whom Wang Lung   35
had spoken said, 'Listen to the young teacher over there.'
Wang Lung listened.

'The dead man is you, the poor people who work hard,' said the teacher. 'The fat man with the knife is the rich people. The rich people kill you to get what they want. You work and work so that they can have huge feasts and rich
5 clothes but you remain very poor.' After this, Wang Lung heard many people talking in this way but he only wanted to return to his land. He did not understand how the rich could stop the rains from coming to the land. But when he asked people they just laughed at him and made him feel foolish.
10 Then he saw something else which he did not understand. One day, when he was pulling his rickshaw, he saw two men seized by a group of soldiers with guns. When the men protested, the soldiers held knives up to their faces. Wang Lung looked at this in great surprise and then he saw more
15 men who were taken away by the soldiers. He was frightened and went and hid in a shop which sold hot water.

'What is happening?' Wang Lung asked the owner of the shop.

'Oh,' replied the man, 'there is another war somewhere and
20 the soldiers need men to carry their blankets and guns. They force workers to come with them. It often happens in this city. I am surprised you haven't seen the soldiers before.'

'Do the soldiers get wages?' he asked.

'No, they are paid nothing but they have two pieces of dry
25 bread each day and water from a pond.'

Just then, they heard the soldiers marching towards the shop. They were coming closer. 'Hide, quickly, or they will take you,' said the owner of the shop. Wang Lung bent down and waited. The soldiers marched away and Wang Lung ran
30 home as fast as he could. He was very frightened and said to O-Lan, 'Now I want to go home. Perhaps we should sell our daughter and go.'

But O-Lan answered in a calm voice, 'No, wait a few days. There is strange talk in the city.'

35 Wang Lung did not go out of the hut in the day because he was afraid of the soldiers. He told his eldest son to return the rickshaw and found a job at night. He pulled heavy carts full

of silk and cotton and tobacco and great jars of oil and wine. It was very hard work and he only earned half as much as he had earned pulling the rickshaw. But he felt safer working at night because he could hide in his hut during the day when the soldiers searched for workers. Wang Lung did not know what battles were being fought or who was fighting but he knew that there was much fear in the city. Each day he saw rich men going to the river with their possessions to get on to ships. These ships were taking them away from the city to foreign places. Crowds of people walked each day, too, to get on trains and leave the city.

Soon the town seemed almost empty. The market was no longer full of food and busy people. The shops which sold silk shut their doors because there were no customers and the city seemed to be asleep. People whispered that the enemy were coming nearer and nearer and everyone who owned anything was afraid. But Wang Lung and the other people who lived in the huts were not afraid. They had no possessions the enemy could take away from them.

Then one day, the managers of the houses which sold silk and wines told Wang Lung and the other workers that there was nothing for them to do. There were no more rich people in the city to buy their goods and therefore there was no work. Wang Lung then stayed in the hut all day and all night. At first he was glad to rest because his body was so tired. But then they finished all their money and he wondered what they should do. They must have food and now even the public kitchens had closed their doors.

'We will have to sell our daughter as a slave,' Wang Lung said to himself. He held the child close to him and said, 'Little fool, there is nothing else we can do.' But, just then, there was a huge noise and a crash. They all fell on to the floor of the hut in fear and waited.

'The enemy has broken into the gates of the city,' said O-Lan. But the only noise they could hear now was the sound of human voices.

Then, from the wall of the great house, came a creaking

noise. A man put his head into Wang Lung's hut and shouted, 'The gates of the rich man's house are open. Come on!'

Very quickly, O-Lan ran after the man and then Wang Lung got up slowly from the floor and followed her. In front of the iron gates of the house, he saw a crowd of people. They were shouting and howling, these poor people of the city. Wang Lung was pushed through the gates with the crowd and through many courts. He did not see one of the rich people who lived in the house. The place looked like an empty palace. But when they went inside, they saw rooms full of food and fires burning brightly. Soon the crowd was inside the rooms where the lords and ladies lived. They all began to seize all the treasures they could see.

Wang Lung took nothing. He had never in his life taken the possessions of another man and it was difficult for him to take them now. He walked from one room to another and then he saw a great, fat man lying in his bed. When the fat man saw Wang Lung, he fell down on to his knees and said, 'Please, please save my life. Do not kill me. I will give you money.'

When he heard this Wang Lung remembered his girl child and his land. 'Give me your money,' he said. The man gave him some gold pieces. 'More,' said Wang Lung and the man gave him more gold and then ran away. When he was alone, Wang Lung counted the money and said again and again, 'Tomorrow we will go back to my land.'

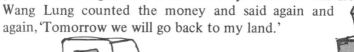
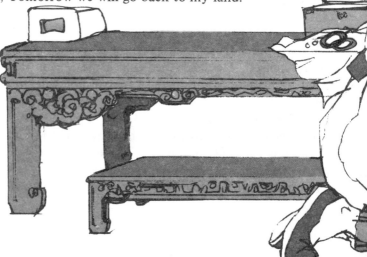

11 Treasure and Land

When they reached their home in the north, Wang Lung and O-Lan found that the door and roof had gone. Parts of the walls had fallen down and all the farm tools had been stolen. But Wang Lung was so happy to be back home that he hardly

5 noticed these things. He went into the town and bought good seed from the south and seed for new vegetables and a new wooden plough and tools. Then he bought mats to cover the roof of the house. Last of all, he bought a new ox from a farmer for five gold pieces.

10 He went into the village and asked the farmers about his uncle. They told him that he was not in the village but no one knew where he had gone. Some said that he was in a foreign place with his wife and children but no one was sure. There was no one at all in his uncle's house in the village.

15 Wang Lung learned too that his uncle had sold his girl children as slaves.

Then Wang Lung started to work on his land. In a few days, he felt as if he had never been away from it and he worked harder than ever before. O-Lan, too, worked hard

20 and tied mats together to make a roof for their house. Then she mended the holes in the walls and the floor. One day, she went into the town with Wang Lung and they bought beds and a table and a big iron pot for cooking. Then they went to a shop and bought sticks of incense and a paper god for their

25 house. This god was a god of wealth and they also bought good, thick, red candles to burn in front of the god.

One night Wang Lung felt a lump around his wife's neck underneath her clothes. He could not imagine what it was. 'What is that around your neck?' he asked. Then he felt it

30 with his hand and found that it was a hard bundle wrapped in a piece of cloth.

'Well, look at it, then,' said O-Lan. Then she broke the

string and gave the bundle to her husband.

Wang Lung tore the piece of cloth and a pile of jewels fell into his hand. He had never seen such jewels before and he could hardly believe it. There were red ones and green ones and golden ones. For a moment, he could not speak. Then he 5 whispered, 'Where? Where?'

O-Lan whispered in reply, 'I found them in the rich man's house in the city. I saw a loose brick in a wall and I knew this meant that there was treasure there. When no one was near-by, I went and took away the brick and found this treasure.' 10

'We cannot keep these jewels,' Wang Lung said. 'It is not safe. If anyone knew we had jewels like this in our house, robbers would come and steal them. We must sell them and buy more land.'

'Will you sell them all?' O-Lan asked. 15

'Why?' Wang Lung asked in surprise. 'Don't you want me to sell them?'

'I wish I could keep two for myself.'

Wang Lung was very surprised indeed to hear this. Why did she want jewels? 20

'If I could just have two . . . ' O-Lan continued in a very humble voice. 'I only want two small ones, the two small white pearls. I would not wear them. But I could hold them in my hand sometimes.' Wang Lung did not really understand why he did it but he gave the two pearls to O-Lan. 25

He thought for a long time about the other jewels. Then he decided to go again to the House of Hwang and see if there was more land for sale. This time there was no one at the gate and the gates were locked. He knocked and knocked and waited but no one came. At last there was the sound of 30 someone walking very slowly to the gates. Then he heard the noise of the iron bar, and an old voice whispered, 'Who is it?'

'It is Wang Lung.'

'And who is this Wang Lung?'

'Sir, I have come to talk to you about a matter of business. 35 Perhaps I could speak to your manager?'

'That dog left me many months ago.'

Then Wang Lung did not know what to do. It was not proper to talk to the Old Lord himself about business, but he had the jewels and he wanted the land.

'I came about a little money,' he said with hesitation.

5   At once the Old Lord closed the gates. 'There is no money in this house,' he said. 'I cannot pay any of my debts. My manager was a robber and he stole everything I had.'

'No, no,' replied Wang Lung. 'I have come to pay you money not to collect your debts.' As soon as he said this, 10 there was a scream from inside the gates and a woman appeared.

'I have not heard that for a very long time,' she said. 'Now no one ever offers us money. Come inside at once.' And Wang Lung went inside the gates.

15   Wang Lung looked carefully at the two people. The Old Lord stood and coughed. He had a dirty, grey satin robe from which hung some old, dirty fur. It was easy to see that it had been a fine robe but now it was very old. The Old Lord himself, who had been very fat, was now thin and he had not 20 shaved. The woman looked quite clean. She had a cruel face with bright black eyes and pale skin. Her cheeks and lips were very red and her black hair shone like a mirror. But she was not a member of a lord's family. Wang Lung knew that she was a slave because of her voice.

25   'Now, about the money,' she said quickly. Then she turned to the Old Lord and said, 'You go away.'

'I did not say that I had money,' said Wang Lung. 'I said that I wanted to talk about business.'

'Business means money,' said the woman.

30   Wang Lung felt very awkward and he did not know what to do.

'I cannot talk about business with a woman,' he said at last.

'Why not?' she said. 'There is no one here except myself 35 and the Old Lord. The Old Mistress is dead. One day robbers came to this house and took away all the slaves and everything in the house. They beat the Old Lord and the Old

Mistress. Then the Old Mistress was so weak that she died. I
hid in a pond so the robbers did not find me. The Old Lord
will do what I tell him.'

'How much land is there left?'

'If you have come to buy land,' she replied. 'There is   5
plenty of land for sale here. He has one hundred acres* in the
west and two hundred in the south. The land is not all in one
place but the fields are large. If you want it, you can buy it
all.'

'But,' said Wang Lung, 'surely the Old Lord cannot sell his   10
land without asking his sons?'

'His sons have told him to sell the land if he can,' she
answered. 'They do not want to live here.'

Then Wang Lung went away to think about what the
woman had said. He went to a tea-shop and asked the owner   15
to tell him the news of the town. 'I have been away from the
place for a long time,' he said, 'and I would like to know
what has happened in this town.' The man who owned the
tea-shop liked talking and was pleased to speak to Wang
Lung.   20

'The most important news,' he began, 'is the robbery at
the great House of Hwang.'

Then he described what had happened and how all the rich
people and slaves had gone except the Old Lord and one slave.

'This slave,' he said, 'is a very clever woman. Her name is   25
Cuckoo and she has been in the House of Hwang for a long
time. She stays there because she hopes the Old Lord will
give her a lot of money when he dies.'

'And the land?' Wang Lung asked. 'Do they want to sell it?'

'Yes,' replied the man. 'People in the town say that they   30
would like to sell all the land except the piece of ground
where the Hwang family are buried.'

This information pleased Wang Lung very much and he
returned to the House of Hwang and spoke to Cuckoo.

'Tell me one thing,' he said to her. 'Will the Old Lord write 35

*acre, 4840 square yards.

his own signature on the contract* when I buy the land?'

'Yes, he will,' replied Cuckoo eagerly.

Then Wang Lung said to her, 'Will you sell the land for gold or for silver or for jewels?'

5   Cuckoo's eyes became very bright and she said, 'I will sell it for jewels.'

---

*contract, a written agreement which has the signatures of the person who is buying something (e.g., the land) and the person who is selling it.

12 Changes on the Land

When he had bought the Old Lord's land, Wang Lung had more than he could plough by himself. Then he built another room on to his house and said to his neighbour Ching, 'Sell me your small piece of land and come and live in my house and help me with my land.' Ching did this and was pleased to   *5* do it.

Now Wang Lung would not allow O-Lan to work in the fields because he was now not a poor man. She worked in the house and made new clothes and shoes for them and warm, pretty blankets for their beds. Soon she had two more child-   *10* ren, a boy and a girl.

Wang Lung felt at this time that there was no sorrow in his life except the sorrow of his eldest daughter. This girl did not speak or do the things most girls of her age did. She just sat all day and, when her father looked at her, she smiled like a   *15* baby. But she did not smile at anyone else. Wang Lung said to himself, 'Poor little fool who cannot speak. If I had sold you, the rich people would have killed you when they found out you were dumb.'

But he did not think about the sorrow of his daughter very   *20* often because he was very busy with his land. He wanted to save plenty of money and prepare himself for the bad years. In the country where Wang Lung's family lived men believed that there were bad harvests every five years. This was because either the rain did not come or too much rain came and   *25* destroyed the crops. Sometimes, if the gods were kind, there were only bad harvests every seven years.

The gods were kind to Wang Lung and, for seven years, there were good crops and each year he paid more men to work for him. He even built a new house behind his old   *30* house. This new house had a large room behind a courtyard and two small rooms on each side of the courtyard. The outside walls of the house were painted white and Wang Lung and his family went to live in the new house. The men who worked for him lived in the old house.

By the end of the fifth year, Wang Lung did not go and work in the fields. He was too busy looking after the selling of his crops and giving orders to his workmen. During this time, he wished very much that he knew how to read and write. He felt stupid when he went to sell his grain and had to say, 'Sir, please read this contract to me. I cannot read or write.'

One day, when some people in the town had laughed at him, Wang Lung came home and said to himself, 'I am ashamed because I cannot read or write. I will take my elder son away from the fields and send him to good teachers so that he can learn these things. Then he will be able to help me with my business.' Wang Lung called his son to him and said, 'I do not want you to go on working in the fields. You are now twelve years old and it is time that you learned to read and write. I need someone in the family who can help me with my contracts and put his signature on them for me.'

The boy's face went very red and then he looked very happy. 'Father,' he said, 'for a long time I have wanted to learn to read and write but I did not dare to ask you.'

Then Wang Lung's younger son came and complained to his father. 'I will not work in the fields either. It is not fair that my brother should sit in a school and learn while I work like a simple farmer.'

'Well,' said Wang Lung, 'you can both go to school, then.' And he sent O-Lan into the town to buy cloth to make a long robe for each of their sons. He went himself to a shop which sold paper and ink and bought paper and brushes and ink for them. Then he arranged to send his sons to a small school near the gate of the city where an old man taught.

On the first day, Wang Lung went with his two sons to the old man. He gave him some fresh eggs as a gift and said to him, 'Sir, here are my two foolish sons. You must beat them and make them learn well.' And the two boys stood and

looked at the other boys who sat on the benches. Then Wang
Lung went home again. As he walked, he felt very proud. He
thought that his sons were the tallest and the most handsome
in the school. When he met a neighbour, he said, 'I have sent
my two sons to school. Now, I do not need them in the   5
fields. I want them to learn to read and write.'

After that, the two boys were not called the elder and the
younger but the teacher gave them names for school. The old
man asked them what work their father did. When he learned
that Wang Lung was a farmer, he gave the first son the name   10
Nung En, and the second son Nung Wen. He explained to
them that the first part of each name meant that their
father's wealth came from the land.

13 The Seventh Year

Wang Lung increased his fortune and, when the seventh year came, he was not afraid. Even when the great river in the north filled his fields with floods, he was not worried. He had enough food saved for his family for this year and plenty of
5 spare silver.

All through the late spring and early summer, the water in the river rose and flooded the fields so that they looked like lakes. Houses which were not built on a hill fell into the water. But Wang Lung's house was built on a hill and it was
10 not harmed. Men went to and from the town by boat and on rafts* and people died of hunger because of the floods. But Wang Lung was not afraid. Because of the floods, he could not plant seed in his fields and there was very little for him to do. He ate good food and slept for a long time each day and
15 then his life began to bore him. His house seemed silent and his father was too old to talk to him very much. He was now almost blind and deaf and most of the time he just sat and thought about the days when he was young. He did not understand how rich Wang Lung was now, and he still
20 complained if there were tea leaves in his bowl of hot water. Wang Lung's elder daughter, who could not speak, sat next to her grandfather twisting a piece of old cloth all day. These two did not amuse Wang Lung and he felt very angry.

It seemed to Wang Lung that this was the first time he had
25 looked properly at O-Lan. He began to think she was a dull and ugly woman who did not care about her appearance. He saw for the first time that her hair was rough and brown and her face was large and fat. Her hands and feet, too, seemed to be growing larger. One day he looked at her and said,
30 'Anyone who saw you would think you were the wife of a

*raft, a flat boat.

worker, not the wife of an owner of much land.' O-Lan sat on her bench and went on mending a shoe. Then her face became very red. She thought he was complaining because she had not given him another son.

'I have been ill since the boy and the girl were born,' she   5
said. 'I have felt fire inside me.'

Wang Lung answered her with anger, 'I don't mean that. Why can't you buy some oil for your hair? Why can't you make a new coat of black cloth for yourself and buy some good shoes? The wife of an owner of land should not dress   10
like an ordinary farmer's wife.' But O-Lan did not say anything and just looked at him in a humble way and hid her large feet under the bench where she sat.

Although Wang Lung was ashamed of speaking like this to O-Lan, he still felt annoyed and said, 'I have worked hard to   15
become rich. I would like my wife to look less ugly. And those feet . . .' Then he stopped. It seemed to him that she was really very ugly but he did not say anything more. He put on his new black robe and left the house.

'I will go to the tea-shop,' he said. 'There is no one for me   20
to talk to in this house except fools and two children.'

As he walked towards the town, his bad temper became worse. He remembered how hard O-Lan had worked in the fields and how she had taken the rich man's treasure. He knew he could never have become rich without her help but   25
this did not stop his temper. Everything seemed less enjoyable to him than before. When he went into the tea-shop, and people spoke to him with respect, he did not feel proud. Even when he heard a man say, 'That is Wang from Wang village who bought land from the great House of Hwang,' he   30
felt no pride.

He drank his tea and left the shop and said to himself, 'Why should I stay in that poor shop?'

He walked in the streets of the town and did not know what he wanted to do. Once he stopped and listened to a   35
man who was telling a story about brave men in past days. But, soon, this bored him and he walked on. Now, there was

a new tea-shop in the town which was owned by a man from the south. In this tea-shop there were many beautiful girls and people played cards for money. Wang Lung had often thought about this place and about all the money that foolish
5 men wasted there. But this day, he went inside the place and sat in its great hall and looked at its gold ceiling and the pictures on the walls.

Day after day he went to the tea-shop and one day he saw Cuckoo there. Cuckoo said she would introduce him to a
10 very pretty girl. The girl was called Lotus and she had small hands, and fine bones, long nails on her fingers and tiny feet. Wang Lung could not believe that anyone could be so pretty. He looked and looked at her round eyes and soft hands. Now he understood why the old story-tellers sang about beautiful
15 girls who lived in past days.

Wang Lung became sick with love. He had worked hard in cold winds and he had almost died of hunger but he had never felt like this. It seemed that he was full of despair and that he suffered all the time.
20 Every day he went to the tea-shop and every evening he waited to see Lotus. All through the long, hot summer he was interested in nothing else. If Ching or O-Lan spoke to him about the land or the crops, he only said, 'Do not bother me about that.'
25 At last O-Lan asked him, 'What is this sickness that makes your temper so bad and your skin so yellow?' But Wang Lung gave her no answer and went into the town again to see Lotus.

Lotus laughed at him and thought he was a rough farmer.
30 She said to him scornfully, 'Why do you wear your hair in a pigtail*? Men in the south do not have pigtails any more. Why don't you cut it off?' Wang Lung did not argue with her but went at once and found a barber's shop and asked the barber to cut off his pigtail.

---

*pigtail, a piece of hair, which is twisted like a rope, and which hangs down over the back of the neck and shoulders.

When O-Lan saw this, she was full of fear and shouted at him. 'Why have you cut off your life?'

'Why should I be old-fashioned for ever?' Wang Lung replied with great anger. But, secretly, he was afraid because
5 he knew he would do anything Lotus asked him.

He did everything to please her. He bought new clothes and would not eat good garlic because of its strong smell which she did not like. Before, O-Lan had always made his clothes but now he went to a tailor in the town. He bought
10 grey silk for a robe and black satin for another coat. He did not want to wear the shoes O-Lan made and he bought black velvet* shoes like the Old Lord had worn. He put a silver ring on his finger and oil on his hair. But he was ashamed to wear these fine things when O-Lan was there and he kept them at
15 the tea-shop. Each day he went there and put on the clothes before he saw Lotus.

Although O-Lan did not see his fine clothes and silver ring, she knew Wang Lung was different. One day she looked at him for a long time. Then she said, 'Now you remind me of
20 the lords in the great House of Hwang.' This made him very pleased and proud and he was kinder to O-Lan than he had been for a long time.

But during this time, Wang Lung was spending a great deal of money. Each time he saw Lotus, she would look very sad
25 and Wang Lung would say, 'What is the matter, little one?'

And she would reply, 'I would like a gold pin for my hair, or jewels, or jade.'

Then Wang Lung would go to the hole in the wall and take out his silver and buy the things that Lotus wanted.
30 One day, when Lotus looked sad, Wang Lung remembered O-Lan's two pearls which she had kept from the rich man's treasure. When he went home, he said to O-Lan, 'Where are those two pearls?'

'They are here,' she replied.
35 'There is no need to keep them,' he said.

*velvet, thick, soft cloth.

'I thought I could make earrings with them one day,' said O-Lan. 'Then I could give them to the younger girl when she is married.'

'No!' Wang Lung shouted. 'Pearls should be worn by girls with fair skin. She has dark skin. Give the pearls to me! I   *5* need them.'

Very slowly, O-Lan look the pearls from around her neck and gave them to him. Wang Lung looked at the bright jewels and laughed but O-Lan turned away from him and tears rolled slowly down her face.   *10*

14 The Return of Wang Lung's Uncle

Wang Lung might have gone on spending his money in this way until all his silver had gone. But, suddenly, one day his uncle came and stood in the door of his house. His clothes were old and loose and his face was hard and brown from the
5 sun. He did not say anything or explain where he had been or why he had come. He just smiled at Wang Lung and his family and Wang Lung just looked at him. He had almost forgotten about his uncle's existence and the old man did not even recognize his brother.
10 'Well, elder brother and his son and his son's sons and my sister-in-law,' said Wang Lung's uncle.

Wang Lung got up from his chair. In his heart he was very worried to see his uncle but he made his voice sound polite. 'Well, uncle,' he said, 'have you had anything to eat?'
15 'No,' replied his uncle, 'but I will eat with you.'

He sat down and took a bowl and chopsticks and filled the bowl with rice and fish and vegetables. He ate as if he was very hungry indeed. No one said anything until he had eaten three bowls of the good food. When he had finished, he said,
20 'Now, I will go and sleep because I have not slept at all for three nights.'

Wang Lung took his uncle to his father's room and his uncle looked very carefully at the furniture and the covers for the bed. 'I knew you were rich now,' he said, 'but I did
25 not know that you were so very rich.' Then he threw himself down on to the bed, pulled the covers over him, and went to sleep at once.

Wang Lung was not happy about this because he knew he would not be able to get rid of his uncle. Now he had seen
30 how rich Wang Lung was, he would bring his wife and family to his house. This is what Wang Lung was afraid of and this is what happened. When his uncle woke up, he came to Wang

Lung and said, 'Now, I will go and fetch my wife and my son. There are only three of us and you will not notice what we eat in this great house of yours.'

Wang Lung could not refuse this. He knew that if he did, it would bring shame to him and his family. The people in the 5 village respected him now and he did not want to lose their respect. In the evening his uncle returned with his wife and son and Wang Lung was very angry. For three days his anger was so great that he did not go into the town at all.

But soon they all became used to Wang Lung's uncle's 10 family in the house and O-Lan came to her husband. 'Do not be angry any more,' she said. 'This is something which we must bear.'

But Wang Lung began to think of Lotus once more. 'When a man's house is full of wild dogs,' he said to himself, 'he 15 must go and find peace in another place.'

Now the wife of Wang Lung's uncle was very cunning. She saw that Wang Lung loved Lotus and thought that there would be silver for her if she helped him. 'Why don't you bring her to your house as your second wife?' she asked him. 20

'But,' said Wang Lung, 'who will arrange this for me?'

'You must leave all the arrangements to me,' she replied. 'It is a simple matter if you have enough silver.'

Wang Lung said he would give silver and gold if it was necessary. 25

Then he waited for his uncle's wife to arrange it all for him. He called his workers and told them to build another court on to his house with three rooms on each side of the court. The workmen looked at him in surprise but they did not dare to argue with him. And Wang Lung did not explain 30 anything to them. They dug the earth and built the walls and Wang Lung bought good tiles* for the roof.

When the rooms were finished, he told the men to buy bricks and to make floors of brick for the new rooms. Then he bought red cloth to hang over the doors and two chairs 35

---

*tiles, square plates of baked clay which are used to cover roofs.

and two pictures of hills and water. He put a new table in one of the rooms and a red dish of cakes and sweets on the table. He was too ashamed to ask O-Lan to help him do these things but his uncle's wife came and helped him.

5   At last, the wife of his uncle came and told Wang Lung that everything was arranged. 'The girl will come,' she said, 'for jade earrings and a ring of jade and a ring of gold. You must also give her two suits of satin clothes and two suits of silk clothes and a dozen pairs of shoes and two silk covers for
10 her bed.'

    Wang Lung was so pleased that Lotus was coming to his house that he hardly heard the woman's words. 'Let her have what she wants,' he said and ran out of the room to fetch his silver. He poured silver into the hands of his uncle's wife and
15 then said, 'Take ten silver pieces for yourself.' At first his uncle's wife pretended that she would not take the money from him but then she put out her hand and took it greedily.

    Wang Lung bought pork and beef and fish and every kind of delicate food that he could think of. It was a fine day in
20 late summer and the house was ready for Lotus. She came riding in a chair and brought Cuckoo with her as her servant. Wang Lung's uncle's wife took her to her rooms and showed her the house.

    All day Lotus lay in her room and never did any work.
25 Cuckoo put perfume* on her hair and oil on her body and gave her sweets to eat. All this time, Wang Lung was very happy but O-Lan said nothing to anyone. She just went on with her work and cleaned and cooked just like she always did.

30   But then there came trouble for Wang Lung. Very soon, O-Lan and Cuckoo showed that they did not like each other. Cuckoo had been a slave in the great house of Hwang when O-Lan worked there. She had often been very cruel and hard to O-Lan in those days and now O-Lan would not work for
35 her. She would not speak to Cuckoo and she looked very

*perfume, a liquid with a sweet smell.

angry. 'What is this slave woman doing in our house?' she said to Wang Lung.

'What does it matter to you?' he replied.

'When I was young and worked in the House of Hwang I could bear her scolding. She was always complaining and I could not argue with her. Now it is a sad thing that she has come to our house and I have no mother to whom I can return.'

Tears fell down O-Lan's face but Wang Lung did not say anything.

O-Lan's anger was not finished. The next morning, she would not boil water for Cuckoo. When Cuckoo asked for the water, she pretended she had not heard her. At once Cuckoo complained to Wang Lung who was angry with O-Lan. But still she would not boil the water. 'I will not be a slave to a slave in my own house,' she said very firmly.

'Don't be a fool,' said Wang Lung. 'The water is not for the slave. It is for her lady.'

'Yes,' said O-Lan. 'I know. It is for the one to whom you gave my two pearls.'

These words made Wang Lung feel very ashamed. He went to Cuckoo and said, 'We will build another stove and I will make another kitchen. The first wife does not know how to prepare delicate food for you and the second wife. In the new kitchen you can cook anything you wish.'

But this did not solve all the problems in Wang Lung's house. When Cuckoo had her new kitchen, she went into the town each day and bought very expensive food which was imported from the cities in the south. Wang Lung was very angry because his uncle's wife was always in Lotus's rooms and she, too, ate freely of the fine food. But Wang Lung did not say anything.

Then one day he heard a scream from the inner courts. He ran inside at once because he knew that it was Lotus's scream. He saw his two younger children had led his elder daughter, who was dumb, into the inner court. Now, when the girl saw Lotus's brightly coloured silk coat and the jade in her ears,

she had put out her hand to touch the bright colours. Then she had laughed and laughed loudly. This frightened Lotus and she shouted at Wang Lung. 'I will not stay in this house if that one comes near me. You didn't tell me that I would have
5 to live with dumb fools when I came to your house. I would not have come if I had known about your dirty children!'

Wang Lung was very fond of his children and did not like to hear Lotus talk in this way. 'I will not allow you to curse my children,' he said. 'Not even my poor fool.' Then he
10 gathered his children around him and said, 'Now go out and don't come again into this woman's court because she doesn't like children.' But he was most angry with Lotus because she had called his eldest daughter a fool and, for two days, he did not speak to her.

15 After this Wang Lung did not love Lotus as much as he had loved her before. He started to think about his land again and wanted to go back to his work. And, one day, when the summer had ended, he took off his velvet shoes and his long robe and his white stockings. 'Where is my plough?' he
20 shouted eagerly. 'Where is the wheat seed?' Then he called to Ching, 'Come with me, I will go out on to the land again.'

15 The Elder Son

Soon Wang Lung was so busy on his land that he hardly
thought of Lotus any more. He ordered his workers here and
there, and they all worked very hard. They ploughed the
fields and Wang Lung himself stood behind the oxen and held
the whip. Sometimes he took a hoe and turned the earth over   5
and, when he was tired, he lay down on the brown earth and
slept. When night came, he walked back to his house and
went to see Lotus. When she saw him, she cried out at his
dirty clothes and did not like him to touch her. But Wang
Lung only laughed and said, 'Now you see that your lord is   10
only a farmer and you are only a farmer's wife.'
   Lotus did not like this at all. 'I am not the wife of a farmer,'
she said. 'Even if you are a farmer I will not be a farmer's
wife.'
   Now it seemed to Wang Lung that he had been away from   15
his land for a very long time. There were suddenly a great
many things to do − ploughing and planting and giving orders
to the workers. When he came home, he was always very
hungry and ate well of the good food which O-Lan cooked
for him. Now he ate rice and vegetables and white bread with   20
garlic inside it. Lotus cried out about the smell of garlic but,
again, Wang Lung only laughed.
   The men in the village all respected Wang Lung and talked
to each other about his wealth. When they spoke to him,
they spoke as if they were talking to a great man and not to   25
someone like themselves. They often came to ask advice
about the marriages of their children or to borrow money
from him with interest*. If there was any argument about the
boundary of a piece of land, they always came to ask Wang

---

interest, payment made by a person who borrows money in addition
   to the sum of money which he has borrowed.

Lung's opinion. When this happened, they always followed his advice.

When winter came, Wang Lung took his harvests to the market. This year, for the first time, he took his eldest son
5 with him. Now that his son could read and write, Wang Lung was proud to see him deal with their contracts for the grain. Once there was a mistake in one of the contracts which his son corrected, and this made Wang Lung even more proud.

Wang Lung began to think that it was time for his son to
10 be married. He did not want him to marry an ordinary girl but he could not think of anyone who was good enough for him. One day he talked about this to Ching after they had discussed the planting of seeds and the harvests. Ching stood in a very humble way and Wang Lung sat at the table.
15 Although Wang Lung often urged Ching to sit down with him, Ching would not do this because he did not feel he was Wang Lung's equal now. 'If only my poor daughter was alive and here,' said Ching, 'your son could marry her. You could have her for nothing at all and I would be very glad. But I do
20 not even know if she is still alive.' Wang Lung thanked Ching for this but he did not say that secretly he thought that his son must marry someone far better than Ching's daughter. Nor did he say anything to his wife's uncle about his son's marriage. He did not think she would know who was suitable
25 for his son.

Snow came and the winter grew very cold. Once again, it was the festival of the New Year and Wang Lung and his family ate and drank very well. Men from the village and even from the town came to his house to give him their good
30 wishes. They said to him, 'There is really no more good fortune that we can wish you. You already have sons in your house and women and money and land.' And Wang Lung looked at his silk robe and the good food and the red signs on his doors and knew that he was very lucky.

35 But spring came and the trees turned green and he had still not found a wife for his son. The boy became very silent and bad-tempered. Then he grew bored with his books and Wang

Lung became very worried. If Wang Lung was angry with
him, the boy burst into tears and refused to eat anything.
'Tell me what is wrong,' Wang Lung said to him. But his son
would not answer. Then he started to hate his old teacher
and would not go to school. Instead he wandered in an idle   5
way around the streets all day.

One day, Wang Lung's second son came to him and said,
'Elder brother was not at school today.'

This made Wang Lung very angry and he shouted at his
son. 'Do you want me to spend my silver for nothing?' he   10
asked. Then, because he was so angry, he rushed at his son
and beat him with a bamboo stick. Although the boy cried
very often, he did not cry at all when he was beaten by his
father. Wang Lung did not understand him and he thought
about him all day and all night.   15

But O-Lan came to Wang Lung in the evening and said, 'It
is useless to beat the boy. I have seen this sickness before in
the young lords at the House of Hwang. Your son is like a
young lord. There is too little for him to do and he needs a
wife.'   20

At first, Wang Lung did not really understand and said,
'But I was not like that when I was young. I did not become
sad and silent and bad-tempered.'

O-Lan waited for a moment and then answered slowly. 'I
have indeed only seen this sickness in young lords,' she said.   25
'You worked on the land when you were young. You had no
time for sadness. But our eldest son doesn't work on the
land.'

Wang Lung was surprised at O-Lan's words, but, after a
while, he saw that she was right. So he said to O-Lan, 'Yes, he   30
should be married.' Then he got up and went into the inner
court and told Lotus about his problem.

Lotus listened to him and then said, 'There was a man who
often came to the tea-house where you met me. He always
spoke about his young daughter who was small and pretty.   35
He said that she was only a child but that she looked a little
like me. He was a good man and he had plenty of silver.'

'What was his business?' Wang Lung asked with interest.

'I am not sure,' replied Lotus. 'But I think he was master of a grain market. I will ask Cuckoo. She is sure to know all about him.' She clapped her hands and Cuckoo came in.

5   'Yes,' she said, when she had heard Lotus's question, 'that was Liu the grain merchant.'

'Where is his market?' Wang Lung asked.

'It is in the Street of the Stone Bridge,' replied Cuckoo.

Wang Lung was very pleased to hear this. 'Oh,' he said, 10 'that is where I sell my own grain. I would like my son to marry the daughter of the man who buys my grain.'

When there was something of this kind to be done, Cuckoo always thought about the money. At once, she realized she could make some money in this matter. 'I will arrange it,' she 15 said to Wang Lung. 'Let me serve you, master.'

But Wang Lung felt he had not thought enough about his son's marriage. 'I have not yet decided,' he said. 'I must think about it for a few days. Then I will tell you what I want to do.'

20   Lotus and Cuckoo did not like waiting for Wang Lung's decision. Cuckoo was greedy for her money and Lotus thought the marriage would be something new to amuse her. Wang Lung might have waited for many days but, one day, his son came home with his face red and hot. He had been 25 drinking too much wine with his cousin, an idle, lazy boy. Now Wang Lung knew that he spent much of his time with his cousin and he did not like this. He went at once to Cuckoo and said, 'Go to the grain merchant and arrange my son's marriage. If the girl is suitable, arrange a good dowry.'

30   Then he went to his uncle and shouted at him about his own lazy son. Wang Lung became more and more angry as he remembered how his uncle and his uncle's family had lived for so long with him and how much money they cost him. At last he said, 'Now, get out of my house. All of you, get out. I 35 will give you no more rice. I would rather burn my house down than keep you and your family in it.'

But his uncle only sat and went on eating and did not seem

to hear Wang Lung's words. Then he spoke. 'You would not dare to send me away,' he said. Wang Lung did not understand what his uncle meant. But then he opened his coat. Wang Lung could not believe it and he stood and looked. Then he was filled with great fear because he saw a false   5
beard of red hair and a piece of red cloth. These were the uniform of a cruel band of robbers who lived in the northwest. They were called the Redbeards and everyone was very afraid of them. They burned down houses and carried off the women and tied up and tortured* the farmers.   10

Wang Lung turned and walked away from his uncle without saying another word. As he walked, he heard his uncle's soft laughter as he went on eating his bowl of rice.

*to torture, to hurt someone and make him suffer great pain to make him give money or information.

16 Enemies

It seemed to Wang Lung that he had more problems than he had ever dreamed of. His uncle came and went as before and seldom smiled. Wang Lung felt very afraid, but he did not dare to be rude to him because of what his uncle might do to
5 him. Now Wang Lung remembered all the years that no robbers had come to his house. He had often been afraid of robbers and put bars on the doors at night. But no one had come. Soon he had become bold and believed that his house and land were protected by Heaven. He had thought he must
10 be a special man of good fortune. Then he had stopped giving incense to the gods and the temple and had thought only about his business. Now he understood that it was only because his uncle was a Redbeard that he had never been robbed. He wasn't a special man who was protected by
15 Heaven. When Wang Lung thought about his uncle, he shook with fear but he did not tell anyone what he knew.

Now he never said anything to his uncle about leaving his house. He even said to his uncle's wife. 'Go into the inner court and eat what you wish. And here is a little silver to
20 spend.' He also gave money to his uncle's son and said, 'Have a little silver. I know young men like to play and I think you should have this money.'

At first, Wang Lung thought about all his problems and could not work. He said to himself, 'I could send my uncle
25 away from my house and I could move inside the city wall where they lock the great gates each night. But I couldn't stay in the city all the time. I must work on the land during the day and then I would have no protection from my uncle. He could easily come and harm me on my own land. Maybe a
30 bad year will come and then even the strong gates will not keep out robbers.'

Then he thought about telling the men in the town that his

uncle was one of the terrible Redbeards. But he knew no one would believe him. Who would believe a man who said something so bad about his own uncle?

Then more trouble came to Wang Lung. Cuckoo brought bad news from the grain merchant Liu. Liu had said that his   5
daughter was only fourteen years old and could not marry Wang Lung's son for three years. Although Wang Lung was glad that Liu promised his daughter after three years, he was worried that it was such a long time.

But Wang Lung knew that he must stop worrying and go   10
back to his land. For a while, the sun shone and the warm winds blew and he worked hard and felt more peaceful. But, one day, a small, silent cloud came from the south. At first it hung in the distance and did not seem to move. The men of the village watched it and talked of it and were afraid. Wang   15
Lung, too, stood and watched it until, at last, the wind blew something to the ground. It was a dead locust*.

Now Wang Lung forgot all his other problems. He rushed into the village and shouted, 'Come. We must fight these enemies who have come to destroy us. They will eat our good   20
crops and we will have no food.'

But some of the men would not listen. They only shook their heads and said sadly, 'There is nothing we can do. It is the will of Heaven that we shall die of hunger this year.' Some of the women, though, ran to buy incense to give to   25
the gods in the temple of the earth. Some of them even went to the big temple in the town to give incense to the gods of Heaven. But the incense did not help. The locusts began to fly over the fields.

Then Wang Lung called to Ching and his workers. He told   30
them to set fire to certain fields and to dig wide moats. They worked and worked without sleeping until they had filled the moats with water.

The sky became black and the air was filled with the deep roar of many wings. The locusts flew in huge clouds on to the   35

*locust, an insect which flies in large numbers and destroys crops and vegetables.

land. They flew over some fields and did not eat the crops.
But they attacked other fields until there was nothing left
and the fields were bare. Wang Lung beat the locusts and
stood on them. His men whipped them and the insects fell
5　into the fires. Then millions of locusts floated on the moats
that they had dug. But, although millions of locusts were
killed, there were many more millions which were still alive.

But Wang Lung's work was not useless. He had some
reward because his best fields were not harmed. The young
10　rice was still whole and good and he was content. Many
people ate the bodies of the dead locusts but Wang Lung
could not do this. It seemed a horrible, dirty thing that the
insects had done to the land. But he said nothing when O-Lan
cooked the insects in oil and his men ate them.

15　Although they destroyed some of his fields, the locusts
helped Wang Lung a little. They made him forget his troubles
and, for seven days, he thought of nothing except his land.
Afterwards, he felt happier and said to himself, 'Well, every
man has his troubles and I must learn to bear mine. My uncle
20　is older than I am and he will die one day. Three years is not
so very long to wait for my son's marriage. I will not kill
myself.'

He worked at the wheat harvest and the rains came and the
young rice grew and soon it was summer again.

17 Changes

One day, after Wang Lung had thought there was peace in his house, his eldest son came to him. 'Father,' he said, 'if I am to be a scholar*, there is no more that the old teacher can teach me.'

'Well,' replied Wang Lung, 'what do you want to do?'   5

The boy hesitated a little. Then he said, 'I would like to go to a city in the south and enter a school where I can learn more.'

Wang Lung was angry. 'This is nonsense,' he said. 'I don't want you to go to the south. I think that you have learned   10
enough.'

But his son went on standing there. He looked at his father with hatred and said something which Wang Lung could not hear. 'What is it that you are saying?' he asked.

'I *will* go to the south. I *will*,' said his son. 'I will not stay   15
in this stupid house and be watched like a child. I do not want to live always in this little town which is really only a village. I want to go away and see other places.'

Wang Lung looked at his son who was dressed in a thin robe for the summer. His hands were soft and white like the   20
hands of a woman. Then Wang Lung looked at himself. He was dressed in blue, cotton trousers and he was covered in mud because he had been in the fields. He thought he looked more like his son's servant than his father. This made him angry and he shouted at his son. 'Now, go into the fields and   25
rub a little good earth into your white skin. Do some hard work and earn the rice that you eat!' Wang Lung was so angry that he forgot how proud he had once been of his son's cleverness. He stamped his bare feet on the floor and spat and walked out of the room. 'No,' he said, 'he shall not go. I will   30

scholar, a man who spends his life studying.

not spend my money in this foolish way.'

Then, for many days, no one said any more about his son going away. The boy seemed to be happy again but he would not go to school. He sat all day and read in his room. But
5 Wang Lung did not mind. 'He is still a boy,' he said to himself. 'He does not really know what he wants to do.'

Now Wang Lung was content until, one day, O-Lan came to him when he was working out what part of his harvests to sell. O-Lan looked old now. She was very thin and suffered
10 much pain. Each day, she got up and did her work but she spoke very little to anyone. Sometimes she talked a few words to the wife of Wang Lung's uncle but she never said a single thing to Cuckoo. This evening she stood in front of Wang Lung. 'I have something to say.'

15 Wang Lung looked at her in surprise. 'What is it? he asked.

'Your eldest son often goes into the inner courts when you are in the fields,' she said. 'He does not work at his books.'

At first, Wang Lung did not understand what O-Lan was saying. Then he understood. His son spent too much time
20 with Lotus. Perhaps he even loved Lotus? The thought made him very angry. 'You are dreaming,' he said to O-Lan.

'No,' said O-Lan. 'Come home early one day and you will see that I am telling the truth.'

The next day, just before he left the house, Wang Lung
25 shouted very loudly to his family. 'I am going out.' he said. 'I am going to the piece of land which is near the moat and I shall come back late.' When he was halfway to the land near the moat, he sat down and said to himself, 'Shall I go back?' At last, he decided he must go back and see if O-Lan was
30 right.

When he reached his house, he heard a man's voice inside the inner court. He knew it was his son's voice. He walked out again and chose a thin bamboo stick and rushed at his son and beat him hard. 'Go to your room!' he screamed.
35 'And do not dare to come out of it!' Then he went into Lotus's room and was very angry. But Lotus looked very worried and sad and said, 'Don't be angry. There is nothing

wrong. Your son was lonely and Cuckoo and I talked to him. There is no need for anger.'

But Wang Lung thought it was better that his son should go away. He went to him and said, 'Put your things in your box. Tomorrow you must go to the south. You will not come 5 back until I send you a message.'

When his son had gone to the south, Wang Lung felt happier. He said to himself that it was good for his son to go and learn more and see foreign places. Now he had more time to think about his other children and look after his land. He 10 decided that he would take his second son away from school and send him to learn a trade.

Now his second son was not at all like his eldest son. The eldest was tall with a red face and big bones and looked like his mother. The second son was short and small and looked 15 like his grandfather. He even had the same cunning expression on his face. 'I think this son would certainly be a good merchant,' Wang Lung said. 'I will see if he can learn the grain trade. It would be very useful for me to have a son who works in the grain market. Then I could sell my grain where 20 he works and he could make sure that I get a good price.'

He said to Cuckoo, 'Go and tell the merchant Liu that I would like to see him. I have something important to say to him and I would like to come and drink a cup of wine with him.' 25

Cuckoo returned and said, 'He will see you today or, if you prefer, he will come here later.'

Wang Lung did not want the merchant to come to his house because he would have to make special preparations. He washed himself and put on his silk coat and went to the 30 town. He walked to the Street of Bridges and stopped in front of a gate. He could not read the name on the gate so he asked someone who walked past. It was Liu's house and Wang Lung hit the gate hard with his hand.

Immediately, the gate opened and a woman servant asked 35 who he was. When he answered, she looked at him very carefully and took him into the first room. Then she went to call her master. Wang Lung looked around him. He felt the material of the curtains and examined the wood of the table and he was pleased. The house showed that Liu's family had plenty of money but that they were not extremely wealthy.

5 He did not want his son to marry a very rich girl because a very rich girl would want too many fine clothes and great luxury.

Wang Lung sat down and waited. Suddenly, he heard the sound of heavy footsteps and an old man came in. They

10 bowed to each other and looked secretly at each other. They sat down and talked about crops and prices of rice. At last, Wang Lung said, 'I have something to ask you, but if you do not like it, we will talk about other things.' He waited a moment and went on, 'I have a second son who is a clever lad

15 and I think he will be a good merchant one day. If you need a boy to work in your great market, I would like him to come and learn from you.'

Liu liked this idea. 'Yes,' he said, 'if he can read and write, he would be very useful to me.'

20 Wang Lung replied proudly, 'My sons are both good scholars.'

'That is good,' said Liu. 'He can come and work for me as soon as he wishes. At first, I will give him his food as wages. I will not pay him any money until he has learned something

25 about the trade. After a year, I will pay him a piece of silver at the end of every month. Then, after three years, I will pay him three pieces of silver at the end of each month. After that, he must rise in the business as well as he can. Because we are friends, I will not ask you to pay me a fee for your

30 son.' Wang Lung was very pleased and he laughed.

When he was speaking to Liu, Wang Lung had another idea. 'Now we are friends,' he said. 'Have you a son who could marry my second daughter?'

Liu smiled. 'I have a second son who is ten years old. How

35 old is the girl?'

'She is ten, too, on her next birthday,' said Wang Lung, 'and she is a pretty flower.' Then the two men laughed but they did not say any more about this matter because it was not proper for them to discuss it any more themselves.

When he reached his house, Wang Lung looked at his younger daughter. She was certainly very pretty and O-Lan had bound her feet very carefully so that she walked with small, graceful steps. But, when he looked at her more closely, Wang Lung saw that she had been crying. He thought also that her face was a little too pale. He took her small hand and asked kindly, 'Why have you been crying?'

'Because my mother binds a cloth very tightly round my feet. She does this every day and I can't sleep at night,' replied the girl.

'But,' said Wang Lung in surprise, 'I have never heard you crying.'

'No,' she answered, 'my mother said I must not let you hear me. She thinks that you are too kind and you might tell her not to bind my feet. Then my husband would not love me just as you do not love her.' She said these words very simply like a child telling a story but they made Wang Lung feel very ashamed. He said quickly, 'Today I found a good husband for you. I will ask Cuckoo to try and arrange it.'

Wang Lung sent Cuckoo to the merchant who was called Liu. Then he sent his son to work for him in the grain market. When his second daughter's marriage was arranged, he felt very relieved and said, 'Now all my children will be all right. Although my eldest girl can do nothing else, she can sit in the sun. I will keep the youngest boy here and he can work on the land. I shall not send him to school. I have two sons who can read and write and that is enough.' Now Wang Lung was proud of his three sons because one was a scholar, and one was a merchant, and one was a farmer.

18 O-Lan's Last Days

For the first time for many years, Wang Lung thought about O-Lan. In fact, it seemed to him now that he had never really thought about her. He looked at her and felt sad because she was thin and old and her skin was yellow. Before this, she 5 had always looked healthy and brown. For many years, she had not gone to work in the fields. But Wang Lung had not asked why she had been willing to stay in the house. Nor had he thought why she moved more and more slowly round the house. He had not even noticed the sounds of pain she made 10 when she got up in the morning or when she bent down to the oven.

Now he looked at her and felt very ashamed. He could not forget what his youngest daughter had said although he knew he had not been a bad husband in many ways. 'What is 15 wrong?' he asked O-Lan. 'Are you ill?'

'It is only the usual old pain which I have had for a long time,' she answered.

Then Wang Lung turned to his youngest daughter and said, 'Take the brush and do the cleaning. Your mother is ill and 20 must rest.' He spoke then very kindly to O-Lan, 'Go to your bed and lie down. I will ask the girl to bring you some water. Don't get up.'

O-Lan slowly obeyed him and went to her room. She lay down on her bed and cried softly to herself. Wang Lung 25 listened to her sounds until he could bear it no longer. He got up and went quickly into the town to find a doctor. A clerk in the grain market recommended a doctor to him and he went to find him. He was an old doctor with a long, grey beard and big, brass glasses and he wore a dirty, grey robe 30 with long sleeves. Wang Lung told him about O-Lan and he said he would come at once.

When they reached O-Lan, she was asleep but the doctor

looked very worried when he saw her. 'Can you give her some medicine?' Wang Lung asked.

'It is difficult,' replied the old doctor. 'If you do not want me to promise she will recover, I will ask you for ten pieces of silver. Then I will give you some medicine and herbs and 5 some tiger's hair and the tooth of a dog. You must boil these and give her the liquid to drink. But if you want me to promise recovery, I will ask you for five hundred pieces of silver.'

When O-Lan heard these words, she woke up and said, 10 'Five hundred pieces. No, my life is not worth so much money. You could buy a good piece of land for five hundred pieces of silver.'

But Wang Lung said, 'I will not have death in my house. I can pay the money.' 15

When the doctor heard this, his eyes shone in a very greedy way. But he knew that the law would punish him if he did not keep his promise of recovery. Because of this, he did not dare take Wang Lung's five hundred pieces of silver. 'No,' he said. 'I was wrong. Now that I have looked at her eyes, I see 20 it would take five thousand pieces of silver.'

Then Wang Lung understood that the doctor thought O-Lan would never get better. He meant that she would die. He took the doctor outside and gave him ten pieces of silver for the medicine. Then he turned his face to the wall and 25 cried.

But O-Lan did not die quickly. All through the winter, she lay in her bed and was very weak and ill. Now Wang Lung and his family realized how much she had done for them in the past. It seemed now that none of them knew how to 30 make the house comfortable or to keep the oven burning. None of them could cook a fish without breaking it or burning it on one side. If small pieces of food fell on to the floor, they stayed there until Wang Lung called to a dog to come and lick them up. 35

The youngest boy did some things to help in the house. He tried to look after his grandfather. But the old man did not understand that O-Lan was very ill and could not bring him his tea and help him get up from his bed. He did not like the young boy bringing his tea and he threw it on the ground. At last, Wang Lung had to take him to see O-Lan so that he

5 would understand. Then, although he was almost blind, he realized that she was ill.

While O-Lan was ill, Wang Lung did not go out on to the land. He asked Ching to look after everything for him and each day Ching came and told him about it.

10 Because he knew that O-Lan would die soon, Wang Lung went into the town to a shop which sold coffins*. He looked at every coffin in the shop and chose a good, black one which was made of heavy wood. The carpenter, who was very cunning, said to him, 'If you buy two, I will reduce the price

15 by one third.'

Then Wang Lung remembered his old father and said, 'I will take two.'

Then the man promised to paint the two coffins black and Wang Lung went home and told O-Lan about it. She was

20 pleased at what he had done and glad he had provided so well for her death. That day, and for many hours every day, Wang Lung sat beside her. He often brought her special food and delicate soups made of white fish and the hearts of young cabbages.

25 Suddenly, one day just before New Year, O-Lan seemed better. She sat up in bed and tied her hair with a cord and asked for some tea. When Wang Lung came in, she said, 'It is almost New Year and there are no cakes or meats ready. I would like you to ask the girl who is to marry our eldest son

30 to come here. I have not seen her yet but I can tell her how to prepare the food.'

Wang Lung was very pleased that O-Lan seemed better. He sent Cuckoo at once to see Liu who agreed that his daughter should come to Wang Lung's house. The girl came with her

35 servant and everyone liked her very much. She was pretty but

*coffin, a box in which a dead person is buried.

not too pretty. O-Lan thought she looked after her very well and that she was careful and correct in everything she did.

For three days, O-Lan was content. Then she asked again for Wang Lung. 'There is one more thing before I die,' she said. 'I know that I will die soon but first I would like to see our eldest son's wedding. Then I can die happily.'

She seemed to want this very much and Wang Lung replied, 'I will send a man to the south today to tell our son to come home. But then you must get better and stop talking about dying.'

He sent a man to the south and told Cuckoo to arrange the wedding feast. He poured silver into her hands and said, 'Arrange it all like a wedding in a great house.' Then he went into the village and the town and invited guests to his son's wedding. He also told his uncle to invite his friends. Now he always remembered who his uncle was and spoke to him as if he was an important person.

The wedding preparations continued and Wang Lung's son came home. As soon as he saw him, Wang Lung forgot how angry he had been with the boy. It was two years since he had gone to the south and he was tall and handsome. He wore a long, dark red robe and a short jacket without sleeves. Wang Lung was very proud of him and could hardly think of anything else. But he took him to O-Lan who said, 'I will see your wedding. Then I must die.'

The next day, the women prepared the girl for her wedding. They washed her and bound her feet and rubbed oil into her body. They dressed her in silk clothes and a light coat of sheep's wool. Then they helped her put on the red marriage clothes. Last, they put powder on her face and painted her face with red paint and put the bride's crown and a veil on her head and pretty shoes on her feet.

Wang Lung and his uncle and father waited with the guests in the middle room. The girl came in with her slave and the wife of Wang Lung's uncle. Her head was bowed in the correct way and Wang Lung was very pleased with her. Then his eldest son came in with his two brothers behind him. He was dressed in his red robe and a black velvet jacket. When this happened, Wang Lung's father understood at last what was going on. He laughed and said very often, 'It is a marriage. A marriage means more children and grandchildren!'

5   All this time, Wang Lung looked secretly at his son to see if he liked the girl. He saw that he did and that he looked happy. Wang Lung was glad at this. 'I have chosen a girl he likes. That is good,' he said to himself.

The bride and bridegroom bowed to Wang Lung and his
10 father and went to O-Lan's room. She was dressed in a black coat and she sat up when she saw them. 'Sit here,' she said, 'and drink your wine and eat the rice of your marriage.' The wife of Wang Lung's uncle brought two bowls of hot wine. First, they drank from separate bowls. Then they mixed the
15 wine from the two bowls and drank again. They did the same with the rice and this showed that they were now married. They bowed to O-Lan and Wang Lung and went and joined in the feast.

All the rooms were filled with tables and everyone seemed
20 to be laughing. Many guests had come from far away. They knew that Wang Lung was now a rich man and they did not want to miss a splendid feast. Cuckoo had brought cooks from the town and they had come with great baskets of delicate food. Everyone ate and drank as much as they could.
25 O-Lan asked for all the doors to be opened so that she could hear everything. She often asked Wang Lung, 'Has everyone wine to drink? And is the sweet rice in the middle of the feast very hot? Have they prepared it properly?'

When it was over and the guests had all gone home, O-Lan
30 was very tired. She called to her son and his new wife. 'Now I am happy,' she said. Then she seemed to fall asleep. When she woke up, she did not know who they were. Later that evening she died.

When she was dead, Wang Lung did not want to be near
35 O-Lan. He asked his uncle's wife to wash her body for burial. When this was done, his uncle's wife and Wang Lung's eldest son lifted O-Lan's body into the new coffin. Wang Lung tried

to comfort himself and went into the town and found a
geomancer*. He asked the man when there was next a lucky
day for burials. The geomancer said there would be a good
day in three months' time. Then Wang Lung arranged that
5 the coffin should lie in a temple for three months until it was
time for the burial.

Wang Lung then did everything to show respect for his
dead wife. He bought white clothes for himself and his
children and white cloth shoes. Their ankles were bound with
10 white and the women tied their hair with white cords.

Then, as if death would not leave Wang Lung's house, his
father died. This time, Wang Lung himself washed the old
man's body and put it in the coffin. 'We will bury O-Lan and
my father on the same day,' he said. 'I will make a good piece
15 of my land a burial place for them. Then, when I die, I can be
buried there also.'

He chose a good piece of land on a hill under a tree. And,
on the lucky day, he called priests from the temple. They
sang all through that night. In the morning, Wang Lung dressed
20 again in a white robe and gave a white robe to every one of
his family. He got chairs from the town to carry them to the
burial ground and they buried O-Lan and Wang Lung's father.

Wang Lung was pleased with the piece of ground he had
chosen. He felt that it was a sign that his family were now
25 settled in their own land and this comforted him. But, when
the coffins were covered, he felt very sad again and said, 'I
feel as if half my life has been buried. Now the life in my
house will be different.' Suddenly he cried a little and dried
the tears on the back of his hand as if he were a little child.

*geomancer, a person who learns about future events by looking at the
earth.

19 Floods

During all this time, Wang Lung had hardly thought about the harvests and the land. But, one day, Ching came to him and said, 'Now that the joy and sorrow are over, I must speak to you. It seems that there will be a flood this year and it will be bigger than any flood that we have had before. Although 5 it is not yet summer, the water is rising up over the land.'

They went out together to look at the fields. It was just as Ching had said. All the pieces of land near the moats were wet and dirty and the wheat had turned rotten. The moat was like a lake and the canals were like huge rivers. It seemed 10 to Wang Lung that there would certainly be terrible floods.

Then the river to the north of Wang Lung's house burst through its dykes* and flowed over the land. When men saw this they hurried from place to place to collect money to mend the dykes. Each man gave as much as he could afford 15 because none of them wanted to lose his good crops. They gave the money to the town magistrate* who had recently arrived. He was a poor man and he had never seen so much money before. There were three thousand pieces of silver. But the magistrate was very greedy and he spent all the 20 money himself and did not have the dykes mended. When the people heard about this, they rushed into his house in great anger. But the magistrate knew that they would kill him and he ran and jumped into the water and killed himself.

Although this made the people a little less angry, the dykes 25 were still not mended. The river burst through another, and then another until it rolled over the land like a great ocean. Soon the villages became little islands. Men watched the floods with great fear. When the water came near their houses, they made rafts from their doors. They put their possessions 30

*dyke, a long wall to prevent floods.
*magistrate, the officer of a town who carries out the duties of judge.

on to the rafts and tried to save some of their things from the floods.

It rained and rained and Wang Lung sat and looked at the water. Now he was glad that his house was built on a hill because the water did not come too close to it. But he was very worried about his crops. This year, there were no harvests and everywhere the people were hungry and angry about their bad fortune. Some people went to the cities in the south or joined the bands of robbers. Others stayed in the villages and ate grass or leaves. Many people died of hunger.

Then Wang Lung saw worse hunger than he had ever seen. The water did not stop rising and they could not plant any wheat. He became very careful about spending money in his own house and he often quarrelled with Cuckoo. She still wanted to buy meat from the town but Wang Lung would not let her. At last, however, she could not go to the market. There was water between Wang Lung's house and the town and he would not allow the boats to leave his house. He did not even allow anyone in his house to buy or sell anything without his permission. When the cold winter came, he told his workers to go to the south to beg or work for money. He said they could come back and work for him when the spring came. Although he was very careful about money, he gave Lotus sugar and oil secretly because he knew she was used to fine food. But, even at New Year, Wang Lung's family only ate a fish, which they had caught themselves, and a pig from their own farm.

But Wang Lung was not so poor as he wanted other people to believe. He had some silver hidden in his house and some gold in a jar at the bottom of the lake. He even had some more gold hidden in the bamboos and some grain which he had kept from the year before.

He knew that there were many people in the village who were dying of hunger. These people hated Wang Lung because he still had money and food for his family. He was afraid that robbers would come and he locked his gates each night. Although no robbers came, Wang Lung knew that it was only because of his uncle's power as a Redbeard. He was very polite to his uncle and his family and treated them like guests in his house. They drank tea before anyone else and they took their food first from the bowls.

Now his uncle and family saw that Wang Lung was afraid   5
of them and they became very proud. They complained about the food and drink which Wang Lung gave to them and demanded special food. Wang Lung knew that it was not really his uncle who complained. It was his uncle's wife who urged him to do so. One day, Wang Lung heard her talking to   10
his uncle. 'Come on,' she said. 'You know he has plenty of silver. Why don't you ask him for some of it? You know that he can't refuse your requests because he is afraid of robbers. It is a good time to ask for money when you are soon to be the leader of the Redbeards.'   15

Wang Lung stood and listened and did not let them see him. He was very angry and tried to plan what he could do about his uncle. But he could not think of a good plan. The next day, his uncle came again and asked for more silver and Wang Lung gave him five pieces. Then, before two days had   20
passed, his uncle asked for more. 'Do you want us all to die of hunger?' Wang Lung asked him.

But his uncle only laughed and said, 'You are a lucky man. There are men near here, who are poorer than you, whom robbers have killed for their money.'   25

Although Wang Lung gave the silver to his uncle once more, his son did not like it. He came to him and said, 'Father, it seems that you like those three tigers more than your own son and his wife. I think we will go away and find another house.'   30

Then Wang Lung had to tell his eldest son about his uncle. 'I hate these three people, too,' he said, 'but my uncle is the next leader of a band of robbers. If I feed him and his family, we are safe. But, if I do not, then robbers will come and take away all our food and money. They may even kill us.'   35

Wang Lung's son thought for a long time. Then he suggested a plan to his father. 'Let us push them all into the water one night,' he said. 'Ching can push the woman and I will push the son. You can push the uncle.' But Wang Lung could not kill. These people were his family and he could not do it.

5   They sat and thought and then his son had another idea. 'Father,' he said, 'we will buy them opium and then more opium. We will give them as much as rich people have. Then they will not want to harm anyone because the opium will make them calm.'

10   At first, Wang Lung did not agree to this plan. Then, one day, he went into the town to see Liu about the marriage of his young daughter. He arranged that she should go and live at Liu's house until she was married to his son. Then he walked to a tobacco shop and bought six ounces of opium. It

15 was very expensive but Wang Lung could not think of another plan to protect himself from his uncle.

    He went to his uncle and said, 'Here is some better tobacco for you.' He opened the jar and it smelt very sweet.

    Wang Lung's uncle was pleased. He laughed happily and

20 said, 'I have smoked it a little but not very often because it is so expensive. But I like it very much.'

    Wang Lung did not want his uncle to suspect anything and he pretended to be careless about it. 'It is only a little opium that I bought once for my father when he could not sleep.

25 When I found it today, I thought you should have it. I am younger than you and do not need it yet. Take it and smoke it when you wish or when you have a little pain.'

    Wang Lung's uncle took the opium greedily. He bought a pipe and lay on his bed all day and smoked it. Wang Lung

30 would not allow Lotus or his sons to smoke any of the opium but he gave plenty of it to his uncle and his uncle's wife.

    Winter passed and the water went away. Wang Lung walked once more on his land. One day, when he was walking in the fields with his eldest son, his son turned to him. 'Soon

35 you will have a grandson,' he said.

    Wang Lung was very pleased to hear this news. He rubbed his hands happily and said, 'This is a good day. Let us go and

tell Ching and ask him to buy some special food for your
wife.'

They sent the food to the eldest son's wife and Wang Lung
was very comforted by the thought of a grandson. Everything
seemed to be getting better now. Spring came and the men   5
who had left the lands returned. Although their houses were
mud ruins, they started to build them again from this mud.
Many people needed money to do this and many people
came to borrow it from Wang Lung. He lent it to them at
high interest and demanded their land as security*. When   10
they had built their houses, the men planted seed and bought
oxen and ploughs. Then they needed more money and they
had to sell pieces of land. Wang Lung bought more and more
land very cheaply.

There were some men who would not sell their land. When   15
they needed more money, they sold their daughters as slaves.
Often these men came to Wang Lung because they knew he
was a rich man with a kind heart. Wang Lung thought about
his large family and decided to buy five slaves. Two of them
were about twelve years old with big feet and strong bodies.   20
Two were younger and could help the elder ones and the
youngest was very small. Wang Lung thought she could look
after Lotus and Cuckoo.

But Lotus did not like the youngest slave. And, when a
man came to Wang Lung's house with a very small, delicate   25
girl of only seven years' old, Lotus said, 'I would like this
slave because she is so small and pretty. I do not like the
other slave because she is rough and coarse.'

'Well, if you wish it,' said Wang Lung. 'I will buy her for
you.' Then he gave the man twenty pieces of silver and the   30
girl came and worked for Lotus.

*security, something valuable which is given as a promise that money
which is borrowed will be paid back.

20 A Great House

Now Wang Lung thought that, at last, he could have peace in his house. 'Now I am no longer young,' he said to himself, 'I don't need to work on the land. I have sons to look after me and men to work for me.'

5 But, once more, there was no peace and again it was because of Wang Lung's uncle's son and his own eldest son. They hated each other and could not forget their hatred. Wang Lung's son came to him and said, 'I wish we could leave this house and go and live in the town. It is not proper for us 10 to live in the country like farmers. If we lived in the town, we could leave your uncle and his family here. Then we could live happily away from them in your own house.'

Wang Lung frowned at this and did not like his son's idea. 'This is my house,' he said. 'If you do not want to live in it, 15 you can go somewhere else. But it is a good house and good land and I shall stay here.' Then he got up and stamped about loudly in another room.

But his son would not give up his idea. He followed his father and said. 'Father, there is the great house of the 20 Hwangs. The front courts are filled with common people but the inner courts are empty. We could rent them and live there. Then you and my youngest brother could come to the land when you wished and I would not quarrel with my cousin.' Tears came into the young man's eyes and he looked 25 very sad.

Wang Lung did not notice his son's tears but the words 'house of the Hwangs' filled him with excitement. He had never forgotten the day when he had gone to the great house to fetch O-Lan and how foolish he had felt then. All his life, 30 too, he had felt a little stupid when he was with men from the town. Now he realized that he, too, could live in a great house and be like a great lord.

He sat and thought about the plan and dreamed about all the things he could do in the great house. Then he asked his second son what he thought about it. 'It is an excellent idea,' said the second son. 'If we lived in Hwang's house, I could marry and live there with my wife. We could all live together like a rich family.' 5

Wang Lung felt a little ashamed when he heard this because he had hardly thought about his second son's marriage. But he did not say this. Instead he said quickly, 'Yes, I have been thinking about your marriage. But, until now, I have been too busy to arrange it. Now that the floods and hunger are over, we will discuss it.' 10

'Yes,' said his second son. 'I would like to be married and have sons. But don't find me a wife in the town. A town girl would always be talking about the fine things in her father's house and trying to make me spend money. My eldest brother's wife does this and I don't like it.' 15

Wang Lung was surprised to hear this because he had not thought his other son's wife was like this. But he thought his second son's words were wise and he was glad that he wished to save money. 20

'What sort of girl would you like then?' he asked his son.

'I would like a girl from a village,' replied the second son. 'She must come from a good family and not have any poor relatives. She must bring a good dowry with her and be neither very pretty nor plain. I would like her to be a good cook. Even if we have servants, she must be able to tell them what to do in the kitchen. If she buys food, she must be able to buy enough but not too much. If she buys cloth for clothes, there must also be enough but not too much.' 25 30

His father was surprised when he heard this speech. He felt that he hardly knew his son. But he laughed and said, 'I will look for such a girl. Ching will help me find one in one of the villages near here.'

Then Ching went and looked and looked for a girl for Wang Lung's second son to marry. At last, he came to Wang Lung and said, 'I would rather choose a wife for myself than 35

for your son because it is so difficult but there is a girl. She is
a good, strong girl and she lives three villages away from here.
She has no faults unless you think that laughing often is a
fault and she has quite a good dowry. Her father would like
5   her to marry your son but I said I could not give a promise
until I had spoken to you.'

Wang Lung was pleased about this. He gave his promise
and told Ching to arrange the matter with the girl's father.

Now Wang Lung went to the town and walked to the great
10 gates of Hwang's house. In the front courts, there were
clothes drying on all the trees and many women laughing and
talking. Children played in the pools and there was a lot of
noise. But then he reached the back courts where there was
no one living. The door was locked and an old woman slept
15 outside it. When Wang Lung looked at her closely, he realized
that it was the wife of the old gatekeeper, the man who had
been there when he came to fetch O-Lan. But he did not tell
her who he was. 'Wake up and let me into the courts,' he
said.

20   The old woman looked at him in surprise. 'I am not
allowed to let anyone into the courts unless they wish to rent
the whole of the inner courts,' she said.

'Well,' said Wang Lung. 'I am that man. I will rent them if I
like the place.'

25   He followed the old woman through the door and walked
through the courts. He remembered them very well especially
the little room where, long ago, he had left his basket and the
great hall where he had seen the Old Mistress. Suddenly, he
walked forward and sat where she had sat. He put his hand
30 firmly on the table, 'I will have this house,' he said.

When he had decided that he wanted to live in Hwang's
house, Wang Lung wanted it all to be arranged very quickly.
Now that he was older, he did not like to wait for anything.
He told his eldest son to arrange it and he asked his second
35 son to help them move their possessions to the new house in
the town. First Lotus and Cuckoo went to the town with
their slaves. Then Wang Lung's eldest son and his wife and

slaves moved away from the land. But Wang Lung himself did not go at once. The thought of leaving his land, the land where he was born, made him sad and he could not hurry away. 'Prepare a court for me to use,' he said to his sons. 'Then, when I wish it, I will come. I will come perhaps on the day before my grandson is born. I will bring my poor fool with me because there is no one else who will look after her.'

He said this with a little anger at the wife of his eldest son because she refused to look at the poor fool. She did not even like the girl to come anywhere near her and often said to her husband, 'A girl like that should not be alive. If I even look at her, I am afraid she will make my child ugly.' When the eldest son remembered how much his wife hated the poor fool, he stopped urging his father to come quickly to the town.

Now there was only the uncle's family and Wang Lung and the poor fool in his house on the land. The uncle and his wife lived in the inner courts where Lotus had lived. But this did not worry Wang Lung very much because he knew his uncle must die soon. Then his duty to his uncle's generation* would be over and he could forget their family and all the trouble they had caused.

One day his uncle's son came to Wang Lung and said he was going away. 'There is a war in the north,' he said, ' and I would like to join it and see some new things. If you will give me silver to buy clothes and covers for my bed and a foreign gun, I will go at once.'

Wang Lung was very pleased when he heard this but he did not say so. Instead he pretended to think about it very carefully. 'But you are the only son of my uncle,' he said after a while. 'After you, there is no one to have children and continue his family. If you go to war, something might happen to you.'

But the man answered, 'I am not a fool. I will not stand anywhere where I might be killed. If there is a battle, I will

*generation, a single stage in the descent of a family (e.g., grandparents, parents and children are three generations of a family).

go away until it is over. I only wish to travel a little before I am too old.' Then Wang Lung gave him the silver and was pleased to give it to him. He felt very happy and he was sure that the gods were kind to him now. They had sent his
5   uncle's son away. Now they would surely give him a grandson.

21 Three Generations

Now there were only his uncle's family in the house in the country, there was very little for Wang Lung to do. He often went into the town to his new house and he sat and waited for his grandson to be born. He walked around the courts and thought about his new life. He still could not really believe 5 that Hwang's house was now his house. He was very proud that they now lived like a great family. He began to buy fine silk and satin cloth and tables of black wood from the south and new clothes for their slaves. He slept until late in the morning and ate delicate, rich man's food. 10

Wang Lung passed his time in this idle and luxurious way until, one morning, Cuckoo told him that his grandson would soon be born. At once, Wang Lung went to the shop that sold incense. Then he walked to the temple where the Goddess of Mercy lived. He gave the incense and some money to the 15 priest. Then, as he watched the incense burning, a terrible thought came to him. Perhaps the child of his eldest son would be a girl? Then he made a promise to the Goddess. 'If the child is a boy, I will buy a new red robe for the goddess. But, if it is a girl, I will not buy anything.' 20

But he was still worried about this when he walked out of the temple. What else could he do? He bought some more incense and walked to the little temple of the earth on his own land. Here, too, he burned incense and he said to the god and goddess, 'My father and I have always cared for you 25 and respected you. If this child is a girl, we will care for you no longer.'

After this, he felt that he had done all he could. He walked back to the house in the town and waited. Everyone was very busy and no one came to speak to him. He wanted some tea 30 to drink and a towel but, when he clapped his hands, no slave came.

At last, when it was almost night, Lotus and Cuckoo came to him. They looked happy and pleased. 'There is now a grandson in your house,' Lotus said. 'The mother and the child are both well.'

5 When the child was one month old, Wang Lung gave a great feast for its birth and he invited all the great people in the town. He bought hundreds of eggs which had been coloured red and there was much joy in his house. After the feast, his eldest son came to him and said, 'Now there are 10 three generations of our family in this house. I think we should have stones put in the great hall like the stones great families have with their ancestors' names on. Then we can worship them on feast days.'

Wang Lung liked this idea and he bought the stones. He 15 put them in the great hall and put incense in a special jar in front of them. The name of Wang Lung's grandfather was on one of them and the name of his father on another. Then there was one for his own name and the name of his son when they died.

20 When the stones were all put up, Wang Lung remembered the red robe that he had promised the Goddess of Mercy. He went to the temple and gave enough money for a good robe. But, as he was walking back home, a man come running up to him. 'Ching is dying,' he said quickly. 'He would like to see 25 you before he dies.'

'The earth gods are jealous,' said Wang Lung to himself. 'They are punishing me because I have given a new robe to the Goddess of Mercy and I have given them nothing.' But he walked at once to his house in the country to see Ching. 30 'Here I am,' he said to the old man. But Ching could not speak or make a sign. Then he died.

Wang Lung cried and cried. He felt that he had lost an old friend. He bought a fine coffin and asked priests to come to Ching's funeral. He himself walked behind the coffin and he 35 made his son wear white clothes in honour of the old man. His son complained about this and said, 'Ching was really only a servant. Surely we do not have to mourn for him in

this way?' But Wang Lung would not listen to his eldest son
and insisted that they should show respect in this way for the
dead man. And Ching was buried at the entrance to the piece
of land where O-Lan and Wang Lung's father were buried.

Now that Ching was dead, Wang Lung found his house on
the land a very lonely place and he went there very seldom.
Although he would not even think of selling a piece of land,
he rented some of it to farmers in the village. Then he asked
one of his workers and his wife to live in the house and look
after his old uncle and his uncle's wife. He took his eldest
daughter and youngest son to the town house, and then all
his family lived together in the great house which had been
Hwang's house.

22 Three Brothers

All day Wang Lung sat and smoked his pipe and he was happy. He felt that there was nothing else he wanted. But his eldest son did not feel this. 'I think, Father,' he said, 'that we should live in the outer courts of this house as well as in the
5 inner courts. Soon it will be my brother's wedding and we will need more rooms. We also need more furniture and china.'

Wang Lung was tired of these problems. 'Please don't bother me,' he said. 'I am tired and I don't want to hear
10 about them. Do what you like.'

The eldest son was very pleased about this and he went away before his father could change his mind. Then he quickly bought more tables and chairs and curtains of red silk. He wanted to make their house like the great houses he
15 had seen in the south. So he bought strange rocks to make special gardens and more plants.

Each day, when he walked through the outer courts, the eldest son saw the people who lived there. He thought they were rough and spoiled the great house of Wang and he
20 wanted to get rid of them.

Soon he realized that it was possible to make them go away. When the day came on which rents are decided, these people found that the rent had been increased a great deal. Now they could not afford to stay in the courts of the great
25 house. They knew very well that it was Wang's eldest son who had increased the rents and they hated him. When they saw him, they said to each other, 'There is a man who is proud. He has forgotten that he is only the son of a farmer.' But, although they complained, there was nothing they could
30 do except go away.

Wang Lung slept all day and did not know about these things. Nor did he know that his son was making the outer

courts very splendid. He had asked stonemasons* to come
and mend the walls and carpenters to mend the gates. He had
also built pools and put rare plants beside them. He had even
bought a bamboo tree from India. The people in the town
heard about this and talked about it amongst themselves. 5
Now they called Wang Lung 'Wang the Rich Man'.
Everything the eldest son did cost a lot of money but he
asked his father for it a little at a time. Because he did it in
this way, Wang Lung did not know exactly how much he
spent. The careful second son, however, knew every silver 10
piece which was spent. 'We are spending too much money,'
he said to his father. 'We are wasting it. We do not need to
live in a palace. You should lend your money and get a high
interest for it instead of throwing it away on rare plants and
foreign flowers.' 15
When Wang Lung heard this, he knew that the two brothers would quarrel about the money. But he said quickly,
'Don't be so angry. It is all in honour of your wedding.'
'But,' said the second son, 'it is a strange thing that my
wedding will cost ten times as much as the bride. Our inheri- 20
tance* is being spent on useless things by my brother.'
'All right,' replied Wang Lung. 'I will tell him that we have
spent enough now and that he must be more careful.'
The second son brought his father a piece of paper on
which he had made a list of everything that the eldest brother 25
had spent. It was a very long list and it worried Wang Lung
very much. 'You must stop all this painting and polishing,' he
said to his eldest son. 'We have now done enough and this
house is good enough for us. We are only country people and
we do not need any more splendid furniture and paintings.' 30
His eldest son was very proud. 'Father,' he said, 'we are
not only country people. The men in the town call us the
Great Family Wang now and it is proper that we should live
in a great house.' Wang Lung, however, insisted that they

*stonemason, man who works with stone.
*inheritance, money, property etc. which is received when someone
    dies.

spend less money and he told his son so very firmly.

'Now go away and leave me alone,' he said.

'No, father,' said his son, 'there is something else I wish to say. It is about my youngest brother. I think it is wrong that
5 he has not had a good education. This is making him un-happy.'

'This is stupid,' said Wang Lung with anger. 'Two of you can read and write. You know that I think that is enough. I want my youngest son to look after the land for me.'

10 'But he cries in the night about it because it makes him so unhappy,' said the eldest son. 'You know you don't need him to work on the land. You can pay men to do that for you. If you expect your son to work on the land, people in the town will say you are mean. We could ask a teacher to come here
15 and then we could send him to a good school in the south. Why don't you ask him what he wants?'

After a while, Wang Lung sent for his youngest son. The boy's face was pale and he looked very thin and worried. 'Your brother says you wish to learn,' Wang Lung said to
20 him. 'Is this true?'

'Yes,' answered his son. But he would not say anything else or explain his wishes to his father.

At first Wang Lung was angry. Why couldn't his sons give him some peace? Why did they always want to change some-
25 thing? Why did even the youngest son want to leave the good land? But, as always, Wang Lung let his sons do what they wished. 'Find a teacher for your youngest brother,' he said to his eldest son. 'But do not bother me about it any more.'

To his second son, he said, 'I understand that your younger
30 brother does not want to work on the land. Because of this, I would like you to be my steward*. From now on, it is your duty to look after the buying and selling of my harvests. You can weigh and measure and deal with all the business.' The second son was very pleased about this. Now he would know
35 exactly how much money the family was making and he

*steward, a man who manages another person's property.

could complain if too much was spent.

The second son was so careful about money that he was even worried about his wedding feast. He watched the buying of meat and wines. Then he divided them into the very good and the less good. He said that the best must be given to people from the town — they would know it was the best. 'But,' he said, 'it is foolish to give excellent food to country people who do not know about these things. They must have the second best food and wines.'

Money and wedding gifts began to arrive at the house in the town and the second son watched these with care. But, even on his wedding day, he was mean to the slaves and servants. He only gave them very little money and, when he gave Cuckoo two pieces of silver, she laughed with scorn at him. 'A really great family is not so mean with their money,' she said. 'Anyone can see that you are only a farmer's son.'

The eldest son heard this and felt very ashamed. His brother's meaness was a disgrace to their family. He was also afraid of the bad things that Cuckoo would say in the town about Wang's family. Quickly, he gave her some more silver so that she would not speak badly of them.

In these ways, there was trouble between the two brothers even at the wedding feast. The eldest brother only asked a few people to the wedding because of his brother's meaness. He showed his feelings towards his brother in this way and by looking at him scornfully.

The trouble in Wang's house seemed to spread to them all except Wang Lung's little grandson. Wang Lung worried about his sons. The eldest worried about the honour of the family. The second son thought only about money and the third son thought only about his books. But the little grandson ran happily in the courts laughing and watching the fish in the pools. Wang Lung was never bored with playing with him and picking him up when he fell down. It seemed to him now that he was only really contented when he was with the little boy.

This was not Wang Lung's only grandchild. The wife of his

eldest son had more children and his second son, too, had a
child so that, in five years, there were seven grandchildren.

In these five years, which gave Wang Lung so many grandchildren, his old uncle died. He was buried in the same place
5   as Wang Lung's father and O-Lan and the whole family
mourned for him. Although none of them really felt very
sorry about his death, they felt that it was right to mourn*
like a great family.

After his uncle's death, Wang Lung took the uncle's wife
10 to the house in the town. He gave her a court of her own
where she lay all day and smoked more and more opium. She
was now very contented and Wang Lung could hardly believe
that he had once been afraid of her. 'She is old and yellow
now,' he said to himself. 'She is just like the Old Mistress was
15 when this was Hwang's house.'

*mourn, to show sorrow for someone's death and to wear special
clothes as a sign of this.

23 Soldiers

All through his life, Wang Lung had heard about war and soldiers. But, except when he was young in the city in the south, war had never come very close to him. He did not really understand what it was, this strange thing men called war. To him it was like the earth and sky. It was there but no one really knew why it was there. Then suddenly, war came near.

Wang Lung first heard about it from his second son. 'Father,' said the son, 'the price of grain has risen because the war in the south is coming near the town. We should keep our grain and sell it later when the price will be really high.'

'It is a strange thing,' said Wang Lung. 'I shall be glad to see a war and to know what it is.'

Then Wang Lung remembered how he had once been afraid that soldiers would take him away. But he knew that, this time, he need not worry about it. He was too old to work for the soldiers and anyway he was rich now. He thought he had no need to worry and he went on playing with his little grandson.

But from the war came many men. They were like another cloud of locusts and they wore long, grey coats. His grandson watched them and called. 'Look, Old One, come and see what is passing our gates.' Wang Lung walked to the gates and saw that the town was filled with men. Each one carried a piece of wood with a knife on one end and each one had a wild, angry face. Wang Lung pulled his grandson close to him. 'Stay with me,' he said. 'These are bad men and you must not look at them. We will go and lock our gate.'

But, before they could walk to the gate, there was a voice. 'Oh, hello,' said the voice. 'It is my old father's nephew.' Wang Lung turned and saw with horror that it was the son of his uncle. He was dressed in a grey, dusty coat and his face was the fiercest of them all. He laughed and called to the other soldiers.

'We can stay here,' he said. 'This is good luck. This house is the house of a rich man who is my relative.'

5   Before Wang Lung could move, the black cloud of soldiers rushed through his gates. They poured into the courts and lay down and drank from the pools. Then they threw their knives down and shouted and laughed together.

Wang Lung was in despair. What could he do? He had no power against so many soldiers with knives. He went to his eldest son who cried out with horror at the news. But he, too, was afraid and he tried to welcome his cousin. The cousin smiled in a cunning way and only said, 'I have brought *5* a few guests to your house.'

'If they are your guests, they are welcome,' said the eldest son. 'I will ask the servants to prepare a good meal for them. Then they can eat well and need not go away hungry.'

'Oh, don't hurry,' said the cousin. 'We will rest here for a *10* few days or a month or two or even a year or two. We are to stay in this town until it is time to go to the war.'

Wang Lung and his eldest son were very unhappy to hear this. They pretended they were pleased but then went away together. Just as they had left the cousin, Wang Lung's *15* second son came running up to them. 'There are soldiers everywhere in the town,' he said. 'They are even in the houses of the poor people. You must not fight them or refuse them anything. If you do, they will kill you with their knives. A clerk in my office would not let them come into his house *20* and they killed his wife. We must give them anything they wish. Then perhaps we will be safe. Meanwhile, we can only pray and hope that soon the war will take them away.'

The three men looked at each other and were very worried. Then they thought of the women in their house. 'We must *25* put them in the inner courts and lock the doors,' said the eldest son. 'Then they will be safe.' They did this and also put the children with the women. All day and all night, Wang Lung and the eldest son stood by the door. But they could not prevent the cousin from coming in if he wanted to, and *30* he often came and laughed in the inner courts.

One day, Wang Lung took his uncle's son to see his old mother. She lay on her bed and slept so that her son could hardly wake her up. When she did wake, she did not really know who he was. This made Wang Lung very afraid. He *35* thought his relative would accuse him of harming the old woman with opium. Very quickly, therefore, he said, 'I wish

she would not smoke so much of it because it is very expensive. But she is so old that we do not dare to argue with her if she asks for more.' His uncle's son did not seem to hear Wang Lung's words or to care about his mother. He went
5 back to his friends and together they laughed together in the outer courts.

For a month and a half, the soldiers stayed in Wang's house. They tore the trees and spoiled the furniture. They ate a great deal and they made the gardens and ponds very dirty.
10 But then, at last, the war came and they went away leaving dirt and destruction in the house of Wang.

When the soldiers had gone, for once, Wang Lung and his sons agreed. They thought that the house and courts must be cleaned so that they could forget the soldiers. They called
15 carpenters and masons and men servants. The servants cleaned and cleaned while the carpenters mended all the broken furniture and the masons repaired stone gates and walls and ponds. Fresh water was put in the new pools and the eldest son bought new fish and more beautiful trees and
20 plants. It was almost a year before the great house was completely repaired and, during this year, the uncle's old wife died. 'Now,' said Wang Lung, 'I can surely forget the family of my uncle and live in peace.'

But there was not peace in Wang's house. It seemed as if
25 the soldiers had left bad feelings in the great house and there was much hatred in it. The wives of the two sons began to fight and to show great hatred. They had a hundred small quarrels. The town wife thought that the second son's wife was a foolish, ugly country woman while the second son's
30 wife thought her a vain city woman. They hated each other so much that, after a time, they would not even allow their children to play together.

Then the hatred spread once more to the two brothers and they, too, quarrelled. Again the eldest brother worried about
35 the honour of the family and thought that they must be sure to be as good as his wife's family. The second brother worried that the eldest was spending all their inheritance. The

eldest was especially angry because he did not like his brother knowing more about the family's business than he did. Wang Lung felt that his house was full of trouble and even Lotus was angry. She was jealous of her little slave because she thought that Wang Lung liked her too much. Each time Wang   *5* Lung came to talk to her, she told the slave to go away.

Then, as though there was not enough anger in Wang's house, his youngest son had a new plan. The boy had spent much time learning but he had also spent many hours with soldiers. He had listened to their stories of war and battles   *10* and he had asked his teacher to give him stories of brave men who lived in ancient times. 'I have decided what I want to do now,' he said to his father. 'I will be a soldier and go and fight in great wars.'

'You are mad!' Wang Lung cried. 'Am I never to have any   *15* peace with my three sons? Good men should not be soldiers. You are my youngest son and I don't want you to go and fight.'

'I will go,' said his son with great determination. Then Wang Lung tried to persuade him to stay away from wars.   *20*

'You can go to any school you like,' he said. 'I will even pay for you to go to one of the famous schools in the south. Or, if you prefer, you can go to a foreign school anywhere in the world. But please do not talk about being a soldier. It is a disgrace to a rich man with land to have a soldier as a son.'   *25*

The youngest son did not answer. Wang Lung tried again. 'Please tell me why you want to be a soldier,' he said.

'There is to be a great war,' replied his son. 'It will be greater than any war there has ever been. There will be a revolution and our country will be free.'   *30*

'But,' said his father, 'our country is free already. What do you mean? Our good land is free. I can rent it to anyone I wish and it gives us all the food and money we need.'

'You don't understand what I am saying,' said the son, 'you are too old. But I must go.'   *35*

Wang Lung thought and thought. How could he persuade his son not to be a soldier? He had given him everything he

wanted. What else could he offer him? At last, another idea
came to him. 'I know,' he said. 'We will find you a wife.' But
the boy only looked at his father with scorn on his face.
'You don't understand,' he repeated. 'I do not want a wife.
5 I am not an ordinary man like my two brothers. I have
dreams. I want to fight in great battles and to win great glory.
I will be a brave and famous soldier.'

    Then Wang Lung knew it was useless to argue with his son
any more. And, one morning, his son went away and no one
10 knew where he had gone.

24 Too Old

Suddenly, it seemed to Wang Lung that he was a very old man. He did not want to do anything except sit in the sun or talk to the little slave called Pear Blossom. Pear Blossom comforted him and he felt that she was like a daughter to him. Wang Lung was very kind to her and, because of his kindness, she was kind to the poor fool. This pleased Wang Lung. Many times, he had wondered what would happen to the poor fool when he died. Who would look after her? His sons' wives did not care about her and his sons were too busy with other things. Wang Lung had even bought a little bundle of white poison from a medicine shop. He thought he would give her this just before he died. But, ever since he had bought it, he had been very anxious at the thought of giving it to her. It worried him even more than the thought of his own death.

'Come and talk to me,' he called to Pear Blossom. 'There is no one except you whom I can trust in an important matter. I am very worried about my eldest daughter. When I die, she will still live for a long time. Her mind does not know what worry is and she has no troubles to make her grow old. I have always looked after her but, when I die, there will be no one. No one will take her indoors when it rains. No one will put her in the warm, summer sun. Now I am going to give you some poison. When I die, I want you to mix this packet with her rice and give it to her to eat. Then, she will follow me when I die. If you say you will do this, I will die happily.'

But Pear Blossom could not agree to this. 'I can hardly even kill an insect.' she said. 'How could I poison your own daughter? No, my lord, I will not agree to this plan. But, I will look after her when you die. You have been kinder to me than anyone in the world and I will do this for you.'

Wang Lung wanted to cry when he heard this. No one had

ever paid back his kindness so generously. 'Thank you, thank you,' he said. 'But I would still like you to take the poison. One day, you may need it. Although I trust you completely, one day you also will die. Before this happens, if she still
5 lives, you must give her the poison.' So Pear Blossom took the packet and did not say any more about it to Wang Lung.

So, day after day, Wang Lung sat and sometimes slept. He knew that his life was almost over but he was satisfied with it. Sometimes he went and talked to Lotus, but not very
10 often, because she was still jealous of Pear Blossom. Occasionally, he walked into the courts where his sons lived. They always treated him very respectfully and ran to get tea for him. Then, Wang Lung would ask to see the youngest grandchild and, because his memory was poor now, he would say,
15 'How many grandchildren have I got now?'

'Eleven grandsons and eight granddaughters,' was the reply.

Then he would sit for a little while and look at the children and ask them, 'Do you study the Four Books?'
20 But they always laughed at him when he said this, and answered, 'No, Grandfather, no one studies the Four Books now that the revolution has changed everything.' And Wang Lung knew that he was now too old and there were too many things that he did not understand. His sons laughed at him
25 and he felt like a guest in their courts.

After a time, he stopped going into his sons' rooms and asked Cuckoo about them.

'Are my sons' wives friends after all these years?' he said to her one day.
30 'They are like two cats who are waiting to fight,' replied Cuckoo. 'Your eldest son is very bored with his wife's complaints. I think he will soon find a second wife.'

'And do you know anything about my youngest son?'

'He does not write letters,' Cuckoo answered. 'But some-
35 times a man comes from the south and tells us about it. He is now a great officer in the revolution there. That is what they say, but I do not really know what they mean. Perhaps the

revolution is some sort of business.'

Wang Lung thought about this for a little while but he could not think about anything for very long. If he tried to think hard, his memory seemed to run away. The only subject he could really think about was his land and he still loved 5 it very much. Although he had left it and lived like a rich man in the town, he had not forgotten that he was a farmer. And, when spring came and the air was warm, he sometimes went and slept in the old house on the land and walked over the fields. 10

One day, after he had slept in the old house, he went and looked at the place where his family were buried. 'I shall be the next to die,' he said to himself. 'I must go back into the town and buy a coffin.' So he said to his eldest son, 'I have chosen the place where I wish to be buried. It is the piece of 15 ground below my father and my uncle and above Ching.'

The eldest son was respectful and said, 'Father, you must not speak of dying. But, if you wish it, I will go and buy a coffin.' Then he went and bought a great coffin, which was made of special, sweet-smelling wood. This wood was as 20 strong as iron and was used to bury dead men because it lasted such a long time.

The coffin comforted Wang Lung and he looked at it all through the spring. His sons came to see him almost every day and brought him fine food and soup. If they did not 25 come every day, Wang Lung complained to Cuckoo. 'Why are they so busy?'

'They are busy with their work,' she replied. 'Your eldest son is now an important man in the town and he has taken a second wife. Your second son, too, is very successful. He is 30 setting up a great grain market of his own.' Wang Lung listened and heard the words but he did not understand what she was saying.

One day, though, he thought clearly for a little while. He walked on his land with both his sons. When they thought 35 their father could not hear, the second son spoke to his brother. 'We will sell this field and this one,' he said. 'Then we will divide the money evenly between us. I will borrow your share of the money and pay you good interest. Then I can send rice by ship . . . '

But Wang Lung had heard the words 'sell this field' and he
5 could not keep quiet. 'You evil, idle sons!' he cried. 'You must not sell the land. If you start selling the land, it is the end of our family. We came from the land.' Then he began to cry.

The two sons held him, one on either side of their father,
10 and each held one of his hands. 'Do not worry, father,' they said. 'Do not worry. The land will never be sold.'

But, as they spoke, they looked at each other over their old father's head and smiled.

Questions

Chapter 1

1. Why did Wang Lung's father say his son must marry a slave woman?
2. What had his father given to the mistress of the slave?
3. Why did the gatekeeper at the great house not know who Wang Lung was?
4. Why did he not let Wang Lung in at once?

Chapter 2

1. Describe the Old Mistress.
2. What did she say about O-Lan?
3. Where did O-Lan and Wang Lung go when they left the House of Hwang?
4. What did they do there?

Chapter 3

1. Why did Wang Lung tell O-Lan not to give tea to his old father?
2. What did O-Lan do during the day?
3. What plan did she make for the time after the child was born?
4. What did Wang Lung do when the child was born?

Chapter 4

1. Why didn't Wang Lung sell his crops as soon as they were ready?
2. Why did his uncle have to sell his crops as soon as possible?
3. Why didn't Wang Lung go and visit the other farmers who lived near?
4. What did Wang Lung do with his spare money?

Chapter 5

1. Why didn't Wang Lung invite his uncle to see the cakes? Who were they for?
2. Why was the gatekeeper more respectful to Wang Lung this time?
3. What did O-Lan find out about the family Hwang when she went into the great house?
4. What idea did Wang Lung have?

Chapter 6   1. Describe the piece of land which Wang Lung bought.
       2. Why did Wang Lung quarrel with his uncle?
       3. What did his uncle want Wang Lung to do for him?
       4. What two signs did Wang Lung think were bad omens?

Chapter 7   1. Which of Wang Lung's crops did not die?
       2. Why were the other farmers angry with Wang Lung?
       3. Who did the uncle bring to Wang Lung's house?
       4. What did they want?
       5. What did Wang Lung sell to them?

Chapter 8   1. How did Wang's family get to the south?
       2. What did Wang Lung learn about the city in the south from the men to whom he spoke on the journey?
       3. What did they do when they reached the city?
       4. Who gave the money to pay for the big kitchen where poor people went?

Chapter 9   1. Why did O-Lan know how to beg so well?
       2. What work did Wang Lung do and why did he find it so difficult?
       3. Why did he feel like a foreigner?
       4. Who was the 'strange creature'?
       5. Why was Wang Lung so angry with his second son?

Chapter 10   1. What strange talk did Wang Lung hear in the town?
       2. Explain the meaning of the picture the man showed to the people in the streets.
       3. Why did soldiers seize men in the streets?
       4. Why did Wang Lung find another job? What was it?
       5. How did he get the pieces of gold?

Chapter 11   1. What was the lump around O-Lan's neck?
       2. Where had she found it?
       3. What did O-Lan want to keep for herself?
       4. What had happened in the House of Hwang while Wang Lung was in the city in the south?

Chapter 12   1. What was the only sorrow in Wang Lung's life?

2. What made Wang Lung ashamed when he was with men who lived in the town?
3. What did he decide to do about this?
4. What were the names that the old teacher gave to the two sons? Why?

Chapter 13 1. What happened in the seventh year?
2. What did Wang Lung think about O-Lan now?
3. What did Cuckoo say she would do for Wang Lung?
4. Where did Wang Lung keep his new clothes? Why?
5. Why did Wang Lung ask O-Lan for the two pearls?

Chapter 14 1. Why was Wang Lung so worried when his uncle arrived?
2. In what way was the wife of his uncle very cunning?
3. What did Wang Lung give to Lotus?
4. Why was there trouble between O-Lan and Cuckoo?
5. What made Wang Lung love Lotus less?

Chapter 15 1. Why did the men in the village often come and see Wang Lung?
2. What did Lotus suggest about the marriage of Wang Lung's eldest son?
3. Why did Wang Lung think this was a good idea? Give two reasons.
4. What fact did Wang Lung learn about his uncle now?

Chapter 16 1. Why had robbers not come to Wang Lung's house in the past?
2. Why didn't Wang Lung tell his friends in the town about his uncle?
3. What was the 'Cloud' which appeared?
4. In what ways did Wang Lung fight this?

Chapter 17 1. What did Wang Lung's eldest son want to do?
2. Why did Wang Lung agree to this at last?
3. What agreement did Wang Lung make with the merchant Liu?
4. What other idea did the two men have?

5. Why did Wang Lung's youngest daughter look pale and sad?

Chapter 18
1. Why did the old doctor not dare to take a lot of money from Wang Lung?
2. What medicine did Wang Lung buy from him?
3. What did O-Lan want to be done before her death?
4. Why was O-Lan not buried at once?

Chapter 19
1. Why did the men in the village collect money?
2. How much money was there and what happened to it?
3. Why did Wang Lung tell his workers to go away?
4. What was the first plan that the eldest son suggested to his father?
5. What plan did they finally agree on?

Chapter 20
1. What did the eldest son suggest now?
2. What sort of girl did the second son wish to marry?
3. Who did Wang Lung want to help him in this matter?
4. Why did the son of Wang Lung's uncle go away?

Chapter 21
1. What was the 'terrible thought' which came to Wang Lung?
2. What did the eldest son want to put in the great hall?
3. Why did Wang Lung think that the earth gods were punishing him?
4. In what way did they seem to punish him?

Chapter 22
1. How did Wang Lung's eldest son get rid of the people who were living in the front courts?
2. What does this chapter tell you about the character of the second son?
3. Why was the youngest son not happy?
4. What new position did Wang Lung give to the second son?

Chapter 23
1. From whom did Wang Lung first hear of the new war?
2. Who came to Wang Lung's house in the town?

3. Why could he not fight them or send them away?
4. What effect did they have on the youngest son?
5. In what ways did Wang Lung try to persuade him to give up his plan?

Chapter 24 1. What was Wang Lung very worried about?
2. What did he ask Pear Blossom to do?
3. What did she say she would do instead of this?
4. What things did Wang Lung not undertsand?
5. What do you think the smile of the two brothers at the end meant they were going to do?

Oxford Progressive English Readers

Introductory Grade

Vocabulary restricted to 1400 headwords
Illustrated in full colour

Grade 1

Vocabulary restricted to 2100 headwords
Illustrated in full colour

Grade 2

Vocabulary restricted to 3100 headwords
Illustrated in colour

Grade 2 (cont.)

The Hound of the Baskervilles	Sir Arthur Conan Doyle
The Missing Scientist	S.F. Stevens
The Red Badge of Courage	Stephen Crane
Robinson Crusoe	Daniel Defoe
Seven Chinese Stories	T.J. Sheridan
Stories of Shakespeare's Plays 2	Retold by Wyatt & Fullerton
A Tale of Two Cities	Charles Dickens
Tales of Crime and Detection	Retold by G.F. Wear
Two Boxes of Gold and Other Stories	Charles Dickens

Grade 3

Vocabulary restricted to 3700 headwords
Illustrated in colour

Battle of Wits at Crimson Cliff	Retold by Benjamin Chia
Dr Jekyll and Mr Hyde and Other Stories	R.L. Stevenson
From Russia, with Love	Ian Fleming
The Gifts and Other Stories	O. Henry & Others
The Good Earth	Pearl S. Buck
Journey to the Centre of the Earth	Jules Verne
Kidnapped	R.L. Stevenson
King Solomon's Mines	H. Rider Haggard
Lady Precious Stream	S.I. Hsiung
The Light of Day	Eric Ambler
Moonraker	Ian Fleming
The Moonstone	Wilkie Collins
A Night of Terror and Other Strange Tales	Guy De Maupassant
Seven Stories	H.G. Wells
Stories of Shakespeare's Plays 3	Retold by H.G. Wyatt
Tales of Mystery and Imagination	Edgar Allan Poe
20,000 Leagues Under the Sea	Jules Verne
The War of the Worlds	H.G. Wells
The Woman in White	Wilkie Collins
Wuthering Heights	Emily Brontë
You Only Live Twice	Ian Fleming

Grade 4

Vocabulary within a 5000 headwords range
Illustrated in black and white

The Diamond as Big as the Ritz and Other Stories	F. Scott Fitzgerald
Dragon Seed	Pearl S. Buck
Frankenstein	Mary Shelley
The Mayor of Casterbridge	Thomas Hardy
Pride and Prejudice	Jane Austen
The Stalled Ox and Other Stories	Saki
The Thimble and Other Stories	D.H. Lawrence